On Great Writing
(On the Sublime)

The publisher is grateful to
Professor Elaine Fantham,
Department of Classics, Princeton
University, for her help in realizing
several corrections made in this printing
based on marginal notations by G.M.A. Grube
in his copy of the original edition of this work.

ISBN 0-87220-081-7 cloth
ISBN 0-87220-080-9 paper

Originally published in 1957 by the Library of Liberal Arts
Library of Congress Catalog Card Number 57-14628

LONGINUS

On Great Writing
(On the Sublime)

Translated, with an introduction, by
G.M.A. GRUBE

HACKETT PUBLISHING COMPANY, INC.

INDIANAPOLIS/CAMBRIDGE

Longinus: c. 213–273

Copyright © 1991 by John Grube

Printed in the United States of America

Cover design by Listenberger & Associates
99   2 3 4 5

Hackett Publishing Company, Inc.
P.O. Box 44937
Indianapolis, Indiana 46244-0937

Library of Congress Cataloging-in-Publication Data

Longinus, 1st cent.
    [On the sublime.   English]
    On great writing (On the sublime)/Longinus; translated, with
an introduction by G.M.A. Grube.
      p.   cm.
    Translated from the Greek.
    Reprint. Originally published: New York: Liberal Arts Press,
1957.
    ISBN 0-87220-081-7: ISBN 0-87220-080-9 (pbk.)
    1. Sublime, The. 2. Rhetoric, Ancient. I. Grube, G.M.A.
(George Maximillian Anthony) II. Title.
PA4229.L5E5   1991
808—dc20   90-49700
                                                   CIP

The paper used in this publication meets the minimum
requirements of American National Standard for Information
Sciences—Permanence of Paper for Printed Library materials,
ANSI Z39.48-1984.
             ♾

CONTENTS

TRANSLATOR'S INTRODUCTION

The history of "Longinus On the Sublime" (to give our treatise its traditional title) is very curious. Its importance as a work of literary theory and criticism, its uniqueness among ancient critical texts, are obvious. It was written in the third century A.D. or earlier, but there is no reference to it, nor any sign of its influence, in any classical writer. It has come down to us in several manuscripts, the oldest of which is dated in the tenth century, in fragmentary form, one third of it being lost. One or two doubtful references may be found in a thirteenth-century Byzantine rhetorician, but it remained virtually unknown until the first modern edition appeared in Basle in 1554. Other editions followed and the book was known to scholars from then on. Milton mentions it in his essay *On Education*,[1] and the first English translation appeared in 1652, but it was Boileau's famous French translation in 1674 which made the first real impact upon the European world of letters.[2]

That impact was tremendous. From then on through the eighteenth century editions and translations in most European languages followed one another in quick succession and "Lon-

[1] (Columbia edition; New York, 1931), IV, 286: ". . . a graceful and ornate Rhetoric taught by the rule of Plato, Aristotle, Phalereus, Cicero, Hermogenes, Longinus."

[2] For a full list of editions and translations up to the end of the nineteenth century, see Appendix D in Rhys Roberts, *Longinus on the Sublime* (Cambridge, 1907); for later works see A. Rostagni, *Anonimo del Sublime* (Milan, 1947). A brief survey of Longinus' influence on English criticism is in Churton Collins, *Studies in Poetry and Criticism* (London, 1905). For a full-length study of the same subject, see S. H. Monk, *The Sublime: A Study of Critical Theories in Eighteenth-Century England* (New York, 1935). More recent works include D. A. Russell, ed., with introduction and commentary, *Longinus on the Sublime*, 2nd corrected impression (Oxford, 1970) and D. A. Russell and M. Winterbottom, ed., *Ancient Literary Criticism: the principal texts in new translations* (Oxford, 1972).

ginus" became the common property of all critics and men of letters. It was welcomed with enthusiasm; its influence was very great and it was regarded as second only to the *Poetics* of Aristotle in importance. Glowing tributes to our author abound. I will mention only two of them. There are the well-known lines in Pope's *Essay on Criticism:*

> Thee, bold Longinus, all the Nine inspire,
> And bless their critic with a poet's fire:
> An ardent judge, who, zealous in his trust,
> With warmth gives sentence, yet is always just,
> Whose own example strengthens all his laws,
> And is himself the great sublime he draws.[3]

Gibbon mentions among the books he read when serving in the militia "the entire treatise of Longinus, who, from the title and the style, is equally worthy of the epithet sublime," [4] and added this shrewd tribute in his diary on October 3rd, 1762: "Till now I was acquainted only with two ways of criticizing a beautiful passage: the one, to show by an exact anatomy of it the distinct beauties of it, and whence they sprung; the other, an idle exclamation or general encomium, which leaves nothing behind it. Longinus has shown me that there is a third. He tells me his own feelings upon reading it, and he tells them with such energy that he communicates them."

The cult of Longinus, as it almost became, lasted into the early nineteenth century, but then, for whatever reason, our author sank back into the obscurity from which he had so suddenly emerged.[5] He remained the delight of scholars but he was little known and little quoted. Perhaps the doubts cast upon the authorship of Longinus (of which more later) had something to do with it. At the turn of the century there was another crop of editions and translations, and these have

---

3 Part III, lines 116-121.

4 Gibbon, *Memoirs of My Life,* ed. G. B. Hill (London, 1900), p. 142.

5 Sir Arthur Quiller-Couch suggests some reasons for this neglect of Longinus in the nineteenth century in "A Note on Longinus" in *Studies in Literature* (Cambridge, 1929), p. 141.

continued to appear sporadically since.[6] For the last generation or so, "Longinus On the Sublime" has held a secure place in all courses on the history of criticism and is represented in all selections of ancient critical texts, though he has hardly recovered the popularity which was his in the eighteenth century and is rarely read, as he deserves to be, for his own sake. Only very rarely, if ever, does he appear among the original texts read by classics students in our universities, yet there are very few ancient authors who speak to us so directly and so clearly.

Criticism and Rhetoric

The rhetorical and purely objective nature of ancient criticism, from Aristotle's *Rhetoric* on, is well known. Rhetoric, it is true, meant to the ancients a great deal more than it means to us. It was, to them, the art of expressing oneself in prose, an art which, as Aristotle said, every one of us practices every day of his life.[7] Nevertheless, public speaking was the highest expression of that art, and since rhetoric, "to speak well on great subjects," [8] remained, through Greco-Roman times, the essential content of higher education, rhetorical

[6] At the time of this translation, there had been no further English edition with commentary since that of Rhys Roberts (see above, n. 2). Reference may be made here to the translations of A. O. Prickard (*Longinus On the Sublime*, Oxford, 1906), W. Hamilton Fyfe (Loeb edition; Cambridge, 1927; reprinted 1953), and T. G. Tucker (Melbourne, 1953). Fuller references will also be found in my article "Notes on the περι ὑψους," *American Journal of Philology* 78 (1957), 355-374. The meaning and synonyms of *hypsos* are there discussed in more detail, as well as certain textual difficulties. Reference to it will be made at the appropriate places in the notes on the translation.

[7] *Rhetoric* 1.1.1.

[8] It was so defined by Isocrates (436-338 B.C.), in whose school the most prominent Athenians of the day received their education. It was his ideal of a general higher education in rhetoric which became the aim of higher education in Greco-Roman times. For his formulation of it, see his *Antidosis, passim* and especially 45-100 and 261-285, *Panathenaicus* 1-32, *Panegyricus* 1-13.

formulas were highly developed, and literature came to be looked upon as a treasure house of successful illustrations of rhetorical figures and other clever devices. Great authors were quoted to illustrate this or that rhetorical formula or figure. Even those critics who were primarily interested in writing rather than in speaking did not shake off their rhetorical training but slanted their criticisms with the rhetorical school in view. There is little doubt that our author was himself a teacher of "rhetoric," but, though he obviously knows all the formulas, he remains their master and they never master him. He is obviously familiar with the usual critical distinctions: that between subject matter and style, for example, and the further division of the treatment of subject matter into the capacity to discover the right thing to say (what the Romans called *inventio*) and the structure or arrangement of content (*dispositio*). He knows that style consists of diction or the choice of words and composition or the arrangement of words, and he has, without a doubt, long lists of figures of thought and speech at his disposal. But how differently he deals with them! Like all the ancients he uses the words "speaker" when we would say "writer," and "audience" or "hearer" when he means "reader." But with him this is only a manner of speaking, though we should remember that silent reading was then unknown, so that even when you read (or, more likely, had a slave read to you) you always *heard*. And this habit is not unrelated to the emphasis which all ancient critics continued to place on sound and rhythm, that is, the music of language, an element in great literature which we neglect to our cost in these days of silent reading.

The Subject

It is largely because he uses the rhetorical formulas without allowing them to dominate his work or himself that Longinus approaches literature in a way that is always personal and fresh, and thus has left us the most original (with the possible exception of the *Poetics*) and certainly the most delightful of all the critical works of classical antiquity. Paradoxically, however, even his most enthusiastic admirers and commentators do not seem able to tell us clearly what he is writing about, and for this Longinus himself must share the blame. It is not only that the traditional translation of the title *On the Sublime* is misleading, as most translators admit, but the Greek word *hypsos* is almost equally so. It was used by other critics (notably in the first century B.C. by Dionysius of Halicarnassus, a contemporary of Caecilius of Calacte, whose work provoked our treatise) to mean the grand manner or style. So we find Rhys Roberts,[9] while commenting upon the unsuitability of the word "sublime," stating that: "The object of the author rather is to indicate the essentials of a noble and impressive style." Now the theory of the three styles—the plain, the grand, and the intermediate—whatever its origin, was certainly a commonplace of criticism by the first century B.C. in Rome, but Longinus is not concerned with the grand or any other kind of style. Many of the examples he gives have nothing grand about their *style*—e.g., in the ninth chapter, Ajax silently striding away, his prayer to Zeus, and the quotation from Genesis. What grandeur there is is of conception, not of expression. The subject of our treatise was well expressed by Welsted long ago when he entitled his translation *On the Sovereign Perfection of Great Writing*.[10] For purposes of translation, we shall be much closer to the meaning of *hypsos* and its derivatives and synonyms throughout if we render them by a quite general word such as "greatness" or "great writing" and the like.

The author himself also contributes to the confusion of his commentators because he gets carried away by his own enthusiasms; when he deals with some particular source of great writing, or some particular aspect of it, he writes as if that particular aspect or cause were greatness itself and the whole of it. As the Budé translator puts it: "Our author calls *hypsos* at one time sublimity in the strict sense of the word,

[9] *Op. cit.,* p. 23.
[10] Published in London in 1712.

at another time simple elevation of thought and feeling, or
again the brilliance of images or the powerful effect of word-
arrangement." [11] This is very true; any one of these factors,
and some others, seem at various times to be identified with
greatness. This is only justified because Longinus is well aware
that great writing is of many different kinds.

What is Great Writing?

He is wise, no doubt, not to attempt a formal definition of
greatness. He does equate it, in the first chapter, with "a high
distinction of thought and expression," [12] but this is as vague
as *hypsos* itself. We are then told that, whereas other qualities
emerge gradually from the work as a whole, greatness mani-
fests itself suddenly, like a flash of lightning. This indicates,
and we should remember it, that Longinus is not thinking so
much of great books (as we are apt to do) or of particularly
successful sayings or sentences (as his fellow critics mostly did)
but of supremely great passages in great authors. This will
become even clearer when he discusses the unevenness of
genius (33-35).

We then get a brief discussion of a commonplace as old as
Plato,[13] whether great writing is due to natural genius or to
art (i.e., training). This is not remarkable for its conclusion,
as of course great writing is due to both, but for the striking
metaphors and images which Longinus so deftly employs. His
style throughout will rise and fall with his subject; where he
feels more deeply, he writes with more care and elaboration;
indeed, some passages (e.g., 39) are almost lyrical in tone.

Here the first gap occurs in our text, and when it resumes
we find ourselves in the midst of a discussion of literary vices
into which attempts at greatness are apt to fall (3). That
particular vices of style are the close neighbors of particular

---

[11] H. Lebegue, *Du Sublime* (Paris, 1939), p. xx.
[12] See ch. 1, n. 2 for the meaning of this phrase.
[13] See *Phaedrus* 269d.

virtues is also a commonplace of ancient criticism.[14] The first three are: *turgidity*, where the very notions and images are bombastic, theatrical rather than tragic; *puerility*, where the words are overelaborate to express an inferior idea; and *parenthyrsos* where it is the emotional tone of the passage that is overdone and artificial. Then comes *frigidity* which is discussed and illustrated at length (4): this seems to reside more in particular expressions which are unworthy of the thought, overdone and the like. And the closeness of the fault to the virtue is underlined by the statement that success and failure are due to much the same causes (5).

With the warning that critical judgment is the last fruit of long experience (6) and that we must learn to differentiate between mere grandeur and greatness (7), we pass to more positive considerations and find a further characteristic of real greatness: that it is recognized by all men at all times, and that the memory of it is hard to efface.

Five "sources" or "causes" of great writing are briefly described in the eighth chapter: (a) vigor and nobility of mind, i.e., the power to grasp great ideas, (b) strong and inspired emotion, (c) the right use of figures, (d) noble diction, which (as always) includes metaphors, neologisms, etc., (e) the arrangement of words. These now provide the framework of the rest of the book, which deals with each of them in turn.

The first is obviously the most important, and it is dealt with at length. It is in his treatment of it (9-15 and 35) that Longinus especially differs from the analytical and rhetorical approach of his fellow critics. Not since Plato had this kind of emphasis been laid upon the writer's mind. The *inventio* which the rhetoricians regularly discussed was a very pallid thing compared to the mental power and intellectual qualities which Longinus discusses in the next six chapters: under it he treats of the *Iliad* and the *Odyssey* (9), the capacity to select

[14] Demetrius in his work *On Style* has a neighboring vice for each of his four "styles": frigidity is neighbor to grandeur, aridity to plainness, affectation to elegance, and bad taste to intensity. The same idea is found in Horace, *Art of Poetry* 25-31.

vital details in a situation and to weld them into an artistic whole (10, illustrated by the beautiful ode of Sappho), amplification (11), the difference between Demosthenes and Cicero (12), emulation of great writers (13-14), and imagination (15), and later he returns again to nobility of conception in a heart-felt passage on what makes writers great (35). We find nothing like this in any other ancient critic.

The second source of greatness is strong and timely passion. The treatment of this was reserved for a separate monograph which is unfortunately lost, so that we have little more than the first brief description. There is, we are told, great writing without passion, yet passion is often a vital and essential element of greatness. Surprisingly, Longinus says that certain lowly emotions, *such as pity, sorrow, and fear,* do not contribute to great writing. It is hard to see what he has in mind, even if it be true that the mere expression of pity, sorrow, or fear does not make a passage great. The loss of the section on *pathos* is by far the most serious gap in our work, and the most tantalizing.

The subject of figures of thought or speech regularly recurs in the writings of critics and rhetoricians; it is usually dealt with exhaustively and with considerable dullness. Longinus' method is worthy of a great teacher. He first takes one famous example, the Marathon oath in Demosthenes' speech *On the Crown,* and shows us, with enthusiasm and detailed precision, what a powerful effect is secured by the use of the figure (16). This is a great piece of criticism. He then discusses the general principles that should guide one in the use of figures, how sincerity and passion sweep away suspicion in the minds of the audience (17). Then, and only then, does he list and illustrate a number of individual figures. This number was probably fairly large, for there is another lacuna in our text, but even in these specific cases his illustrations are lively and his descriptions to the point. His description of hyperbaton in Demosthenes (22), for example, will delight anyone who has ever struggled with the involved sentences of that orator. There is probably no other discussion of figures in ancient texts where we actually wish that we had more of it!

A good deal of the section on diction is lost. All that remains is a vigorous statement of its importance (30), a sensible suggestion that vulgarisms can be redeemed by their expressiveness (31), and a refusal to limit the number of metaphors in descriptive passages (32). The chief illustration of this point is a long passage from Plato's *Timaeus*, though Longinus admits that elsewhere there is sometimes good reason to condemn the more farfetched Platonic metaphors.

This mention of faults in Plato, and of Caecilius' preference for the impeccable Lysias as the greater writer,[15] leads to what is formally a digression but actually one of the most attractive sections of the whole treatise (33-36). To Longinus, the greatness of genius with all its faults is always to be preferred to the impeccable second rate. It may be that the truly great lack many secondary virtues, as in the case of Demosthenes, but he is still greater than Hyperides, who has them all; or a genius like Plato can at times be extremely careless. Yet both Plato and Demosthenes are to be ranked among the demigods of literature. Here Longinus is rebelling against the whole rhetorical approach to literature which was prevalent throughout the Greco-Roman centuries. When criticism concentrates its attention on the correct use of rhetorical rules and techniques, on sentence structure, rhythm, figures, and the rest, it dwells almost exclusively upon particular phrases, figures, sentences, and expressions, and loses sight of the more general excellences. It is apt to attach great importance to faults and

[15] Such criticism of Plato was not uncommon. Dionysius of Halicarnassus regularly criticizes his poetical and theatrical diction, though he regards him as a master in word-arrangement. See especially his *Letter to Pompey* 2 and *Demosthenes* 5-7. Caecilius' preference for Lysias seems to mark him as an "Atticist," for those who in the first century B.C. tried to revive the pure Attic manner were for the most part devotees of the simple style. Lysias (459-390 B.C.) was their model, and they accused of "Asianism" anyone (including Cicero) who wrote or spoke in the grand manner. The best statement of the Atticism-Asianism controversy is still Wilamowitz' "Asianismus und Atticismus" in *Hermes* 35 (1900), 1-52.

felicities of detail. This ancient criticism did to an astounding
degree, and it is this whole outlook that Longinus is by impli-
cation attacking here, as indeed throughout. Detailed criticism
of words, figures, metaphors has its place, but he, of all post-
Aristotelian critics, is the only one who keeps it in its place.
This is why he can make a more direct appeal to the modern
reader.

After this digression, we are still in the field of diction.
Another lacuna occurs and we resume in the middle of a discussion of hyperbole. Like metaphor, this was discussed under
diction. Again, Longinus refuses to judge a particular hyperbole as a thing in itself, and insists that it cannot be properly
appreciated apart from the whole passage, its emotional tone,
and its total effect.

Finally we come to the fifth source of greatness, word-
arrangement or composition (39-42). This, our author tells
us, he has dealt with in two other published works. He therefore confines himself here to some general observations and
discusses word-arrangement from the point of view of rhythm,
that music of language to which the Greeks were so very sensi-
tive. Once more an old commonplace of criticism is clothed
with new freshness in a passage of lyrical prose, itself most
carefully composed. Beautiful language, we are told, is music,
but music which expresses thought and which therefore appeals not only to man's emotions but to his mind as well.
There follows a detailed analysis of a sentence of Demosthenes to show that the addition or subtraction of a single
syllable alters the whole rhythm for the worse. Here again we
find that characteristic combination of general principles and
detailed illustration which is one of the main attractions of
our treatise. Like all the other critics, Longinus strongly
objects to short, tripping, and monotonous rhythms and the
cut-up clauses that usually embody them (42).[16]

The last chapter but one goes back to diction and shows
how a trivial word or thought can spoil the effect of a whole

16 For other discussions of rhythm see, for example, Dionysius, *Composition* 17-18, Cicero, *Orator* 168-226, and Quintilian 9. 4. 45-147.

passage. Then comes a curious last chapter, abruptly introduced, on the contemporary decay of eloquence. It has no connection with what precedes, or with the discussion of passion
which was to follow. "A recent philosopher" is quoted as arguing that this decay is due to the loss of liberty and of that
freedom which was the mother of eloquence. Longinus then
replies that the decay of eloquence is rather due to the immorality of the times and above all to the relentless pursuit
of wealth which brings so many vices in its train. This passage has often been praised for its Platonic moral fervor and
its magnificence of style. But it does not quite leave the same
impression of sincere enthusiasm as the earlier elaborated passages do, and it reads more like an academic exercise in elaboration upon a well-worn theme. One wonders whether the
opposition to the "philosopher's" attack upon autocracy is
not partly ironical, even though the condemnation of the contemporary desire for wealth may be seriously meant. Any such
feeling is, of course, subjective; we cannot be sure, but especially Longinus' reply seems to me at least rather too rhetorical
to ring quite true.

Date and Author

I have so far called our author Longinus and made no
reference to his date. Longinus is known to history as a great
critic, scholar, and teacher of "rhetoric" of the third century
A.D. He was a friend and teacher of Porphyry, the disciple
of Plotinus. He wrote a great many literary works but his
treatise *On Great Writing* does not occur in the list we are
given of them. Men called him "a living library and a walking
museum" (institute of higher studies); he was, we are told, a
strong proponent of the great classical writers, and his opinions on literature carried great weight. He was called the most
distinguished scholar of his day.[17] Educated at Alexandria, he
seems to have taught for a while in Athens and then gone to

[17] See Eunapius, *Lives of the Philosophers* 456 and Porphyry, *Life of
Plotinus* 19-21.

Asia Minor where he became the adviser of Zenobia, queen of
Palmyra. Implicated with her in a conspiracy against the im-
perial power of Rome, he was executed by order of the em-
peror Aurelian in A.D. 273.

Until early in the nineteenth century, no one doubted that
this Longinus was the author of the treatise *On the Sublime*. True, his name was Cassius Longinus whereas our
manuscripts gave the author's name as Dionysius Longinus,
but it was not unknown for Greeks to take Roman names as
well as their own. At any rate, not much attention was paid
to this discrepancy until it was suddenly discovered that a
reference in the index of our oldest manuscript (not the actual
title) spoke of "Dionysius *or* Longinus" as the author. A similar reference was found in one or two other manuscripts and
one spoke of the author as unknown. Clearly, the argument
now ran, the author *was* unknown and some Byzantine scribe
thought that he must be one of the two great critics, either
Dionysius of Halicarnassus in the first century A.D. or Cassius
Longinus in the third, and entitled the work accordingly.
This is possible, but it is not such a very natural guess, for
there were other famous critics. Things might well have
happened the other way around: faced with an unknown
Dionysius Longinus (and knowing Cassius only) the mythical Byzantine might well have thought this must have meant
either Dionysius *or* Longinus and acted accordingly. In the
realm of complete uncertainty, one guess is as good as another.
We may note that in any case the name Dionysius has certainly
no more authority behind it than the name Longinus, and it is
ironic to find scholars who reject Longinus' authorship yet
attribute the work to four different Dionysii! [18]

There is little external evidence. The "Dionysius Longinus"
of even later manuscripts *might* represent an independent tra-
dition. There are two interesting references in John of Sicily

18 The various guesses as to authorship are discussed by Rhys Roberts,
where the fullest argument against the Longinian authorship will be
found. On the other side see Churton Collins, *op. cit.*

(13th century) who says [19] that the historical Longinus spoke with respect of Moses, and condemned Aeschylus for bombast in his *Philological Discussions*. Both these opinions occur in the ninth chapter of our treatise and, unless the author is the same, this is certainly a strange coincidence. Indeed, our treatise might possibly *be* that part of the *Philological Discussions*.

It is nowadays fashionable to date *On Great Writing* in the first century A.D. There are two arguments in favor of this date, neither very convincing: first, that our author is answering Caecilius of Calacte whom we know to have lived in Rome in the first century B.C.; second, that the decay of eloquence, the subject of our last chapter, was much discussed in the first century A.D. It can be pointed out, however, that the works of Caecilius were classics of literary criticism; Plutarch rebukes him (about A.D. 100) for his indiscretion in writing a comparison of the style of Demosthenes and Cicero;[20] obviously the works of Caecilius would be studied by such "a walking library" as Longinus a hundred and fifty years later and a work on a subject of special interest to him might well provoke him to write on the same subject. This was not unusual. The rhetorical works of Hermogenes (2nd century A.D.) continued to be annotated and commented on for centuries, and many of these commentaries are extant.

As for the last chapter, it is quite true that the decay of eloquence was a favorite topic of discussion in the first century of the empire, as we know from Seneca the Elder, Petronius, Tacitus and others. Indeed, by the time of Quintilian (*c.* A.D. 90) who wrote on the subject, it was already a commonplace. Even if we do not have another such outburst from the third century, it is hardly likely that men stopped talking about the good old days. For a man like Longinus who, we are specifically told, concentrated on "the criticism of the ancients" the subject was a very natural one.

There are no other arguments of any importance to sup-

---

[19] See Walz, *Rhetores Graeci*, VI, 211, 225; VII, 963.
[20] Plutarch, *Life of Demosthenes* 3.

port either date or authorship. It is not true, for example, as has been said, that the style and mental power of our author are completely incompatible with those of the *Art of Rhetoric* by Longinus which we also possess. And in this connection it is amusing to remember that this same *Art of Rhetoric* was in fact preserved among the works of another rhetorician, Apsines, and was first extracted therefrom by the German scholar Ruhnken about two centuries ago because its manner and style so vividly reminded him of the author of *On the Sublime!* [21]

Certainty is of course impossible. But we can be sure of one thing: this treatise is so different from any other we possess that no other critic whose works we do have could possibly have written it. It may have been written by someone of whom we know only the name, but that kind of guess is quite unprofitable. The only reasonable conclusion is that it was either written by Cassius Longinus, for it contradicts nothing we know of him, or by someone else we know nothing about, whom we may then as well call Dionysius Longinus. In that case the greatest of Greco-Roman critics is otherwise totally unknown to us from any other source.

In the case of a work of real genius like this, the date is of very secondary importance; the author's critical principles do not fit in with those of any known school.[22] It is, indeed, his

21 See Churton Collins, *op. cit.*, p. 240 n.

22 It has been suggested that our author belonged to the school of Theodorus of Gadara, a contemporary of Tiberius, and was indeed a younger contemporary and direct disciple. Rostagni even goes so far in his recent edition (see above, n. 2) as to identify him with one Hermagoras mentioned as such by Quintilian (3. 1. 17).

This novel identification can be no more than an attractive guess. The theory that our author was a younger contemporary of Theodorus relies very heavily upon the use of the imperfect in ch. 3: ". . . a third error. Theodorus *used to call it* ($\dot{\epsilon}\kappa\acute{a}\lambda\epsilon\iota$) parenthyrsos." But the imperfect need only mean that Theodorus originated the term and used it more than once. An exact parallel is found in Demetrius *On Style* (76), where we are told that the fourth-century B.C. painter Nicias "used to say" ($\ddot{\epsilon}\lambda\epsilon\gamma\epsilon\nu$) that the choice of subject was an important part of the art of painting, but

free and unique critical attitude that makes his work valuable, not only for its influence in past centuries, but for itself. As a critic he is still the Longinus

> Whose own example strengthens all his laws
> And is himself the great sublime he draws.

G. M. A. GRUBE

---

that use of the imperfect has not prevented modern scholars from dating *On Style* in the first century A.D.

The possible dependence of our author upon Theodorus *and his followers* is of greater interest, as it involves the whole question of the nature of the rivalry between that school and that of Apollodorus of Pergamum. The evidence will be found in M. Schanz' article, "Die Apollodoreer und die Theodoreer" in *Hermes* 35 (1890), 36-54, and in H. Mutschmann's attractive book, *Tendenz, Aufbau und Quellen der Schrift vom Erhabenen* (Berlin, 1913), pp. 46-70. Schanz challenged the opinion, derived from Quintilian, that the differences between the two schools were restricted to technical minutiae, and he shows that there was a principle involved. Apollodorus was far more rigid: he insisted that every speech had to have the same four parts, in the same order, and so on; Theodorus was less rigid, more adaptable, acknowledging that a part might be omitted in certain cases, etc. To Theodorus rhetoric was a *technê*, while to Apollodorus it was an exact science. Mutschmann goes further and tries to prove that Theodorus attached far more importance to pathos, to the irrational element and the imagination, in rhetoric and in literature. He then finds some parallels in our treatise which convince him that its author drew heavily on Theodorean sources and indeed derived from them the importance he places on the first two sources of the sublime. Rostagni goes further still and makes Theodorus into a kind of apostle of the irrational in literature.

The problem cannot be argued in detail here. Suffice it to say that while it is quite likely that our author drew upon Theodorean sources as he did on many others, the direct relationship with Theodorus himself is certainly not proved. I am not convinced that the picture of Theodorus drawn by Mutschmann and elaborated by Rostagni is historically sound. On the contrary, it seems that the ideas that can be traced to Theodorus may well have been restricted in their application to rhetorical technicalities—the theory of the parts of speech, etc.—which would agree with the definite impression we get from Quintilian, our best authority. Some of Theodorus' followers may have applied them more widely, but the relation of our author to Theodorus himself was not, in my opinion, at all close, certainly not close enough to prove him a direct disciple or to affect the date of our treatise.

NOTE ON THE TEXT

The text of Longinus is fairly well established, and the different readings are not very important, with one or two exceptions. This translation is based on A. O. Prickard's Oxford text (1906). No new readings have been adopted, but rather an effort has been made to retain the readings of the Mss., even where, as in the first sentence of ch. 35, an old emendation (ὁ Λυσίας for ἀπουσίας) has been generally accepted. Other passages where there is a difference, not of text but of interpretation, are in ch. 7 (the meaning of *anathêma*), the last sentence of ch. 10, and the meaning of *periodos* at the beginning of chs. 11 and 40. None of these, except the first (in ch. 35) makes any very significant difference of meaning. All these passages, some other textual problems, and the true meaning of *hypsos* itself, are fully discussed in "Notes on the περὶ ὕψους" in the *American Journal of Philology* 78 (1957), 355-374. For notice of other editions and translations see notes 2 and 6 of the Introduction.

G. M. A. G.

ON GREAT WRITING

(On the Sublime)

LONGINUS ON GREAT WRITING
(On the Sublime)

1

When you and I, my dear Postumius Terentianus, studied Caecilius' monograph on Great Writing together,[1] we felt, as you know, that it was not worthy of its subject, failed to touch the essential points, and gave little help to the reader, which surely an author should aim to do above all else. Two things are required from every specialized treatise: it should clarify its subject and, in the second place, but actually more important, it should tell us how and by what methods we can attain it and make it ours. Now Caecilius does try to show what great writing is—as if we did not know it!—and gives a great many examples, but he somehow fails to tell us how we can strengthen our natural talents and to some extent acquire greatness. This he omits as if it were superfluous. However, we should perhaps not blame the man for what he does not say but rather praise him for his intention and his earnestness.

Since you requested that I too should produce some commentary on great writing as a favor to you, let us see whether our study has led to anything which may be useful to public speakers. You, as befits a man of your talents, will help me with frank criticism of the points I am about to make, for indeed it was well said that what we have in common with the gods is kindly service and truthfulness.

In writing to a scholar like yourself, my dear friend, there is no need for me to begin by establishing at length that

[1] For the meaning of the word *hypsos* and its derivatives, i.e., the subject of the treatise, see Introduction, pp. xi-xii, and *AJP* 78 (1957), 355-360. Terentianus is quite unknown.

great passages have a high distinction of thought and expression [2] to which great writers owe their supremacy and their
lasting renown. Great writing does not persuade; it takes
the reader out of himself. The startling and amazing is more
powerful than the charming and persuasive, if it is indeed true
that to be convinced is usually within our control whereas
amazement is the result of an irresistible force beyond the
control of any audience. We become aware of a writer's inven-
tive skill, the structure and arrangement of his subject matter, not from one or two passages, but as these qualities slowly
emerge from the texture of the whole work. But greatness
appears suddenly; like a thunderbolt it carries all before it
and reveals the writer's full power in a flash. These reflections
and others of the same kind, my dear Terentianus, you could
yourself supply out of your own experience.

2

The first problem we have to face is whether greatness and
depth [1] in literature is a matter of art.[2] Some people main-

[2] The Greek word *logos,* either in the singular or the plural, can refer
to the content of a passage (what is being said) or to the language in
which it is said, or both. It is here usually translated as the second, i.e.,
"distinction of *language"* or the like. This I believe mistaken, for we find
later that diction or the choice of *words* is but one of the five sources of
greatness (ch. 8) and Longinus puts a great deal of emphasis on the mind
of the writer throughout; indeed, the thought alone, without its expression, may be sufficient. *Logos* therefore refers here to both thought and
expression, and I have used both words to translate it, for both ideas, I
am sure, are in the writer's mind.

[1] The Greek word *bathos* means "depth," and so most translators render it. The new edition of Liddell, Scott, Jones, *Greek-English Lexicon*
(Oxford, 1940) still takes it as "bathos," but for this meaning there is no
authority. See *AJP* 78 (1957), 360-362.

[2] The word *techné,* here translated "art," means more than "technique"
but is perhaps more restricted in meaning than "art." It implies theory
and training and is easily contrasted to natural talent, as here. Any art or
craft is a *techné*—farming, building, medicine as well as the fine arts,
poetry and prose: anything, in fact, which requires special knowledge and
training. A rhetorical textbook was called a *techné,* and in Latin an *ars.*

tain that to bring such things under technical rules is merely to deceive oneself. "Great writers are born, not made," says our author,[3] "and there is only one kind of art: to be born with talent." The products of nature are thought to be enfeebled and debased when reduced to dry bones by systematic precepts. But I say that this will be proved otherwise if one considers that natural talent, though generally a law unto itself in passionate and distinguished passages, is not usually random or altogether devoid of method. Nature supplies the first main underlying elements in all cases, but study enables one to define the right moment and appropriate measure on each occasion, and also provides steady training and practice.

Great qualities are too precarious when left to themselves, unsteadied and unballasted by knowledge, abandoned to mere impulse and untutored daring; they need the bridle as well as the spur. Demosthenes shows that this is true in everyday life when he says that while the greatest blessing is good fortune, the second, no less important, is good counsel, and that the absence of the second utterly destroys the first. We might apply this to literature, with talent in the place of fortune and art in that of counsel. The clinching proof is that only by means of art can we perceive the fact that certain literary effects are due to sheer inborn talent. If, as I said, those who object to literary criticism would ponder these things, they would, I think, no longer consider the investigation of our subject extravagant or useless.

.   .   .   .

3

    . . . the hearth's tall flames be quenched.
And, should I see a single householder,
I'll weave a coronal of torrential fire,
Burn down the roof, consume it all to ashes.
No noble utterance have I spoken yet.

[3] Presumably Caecilius, but Longinus uses the expressions "says he" or "say they" in a vague manner, and the reference is often far from clear.

These expressions [1] are not tragic but theatrical: I mean the coronals, the spewing up to heaven, the image of Boreas playing the flute, and all the rest. The result is not forcefulness but turgidity of language and confusion of images. Examined in a clear light, the passage sinks from being awe-inspiring to triviality. If incongruous turgidity is unforgivable in tragedy, a naturally dignified genre which even admits some bombast, it can hardly be suitable in a discourse which deals with facts.

So people laugh at the expressions used by Gorgias of Leontini, such as his "Xerxes, the Zeus of the Persians" and "the vultures, living graves"; also at some phrases of Callisthenes which are not elevated but up in the air. They laugh even more at Cleitarchus, a superficial writer who, in the words of Sophocles, "puffs on a small flute without any stops." [2] Amphicrates, Hegesias, and Matris do the same thing; they often believe themselves inspired, but theirs is no Bacchic frenzy; they are triflers.

Turgidity seems to be one of the most difficult faults to avoid, for those who aim at greatness try to escape the charge of feeble aridity and are somehow led into turgidity, believing it "a noble error to fail in great things." As in the body, so in writing, hollow and artificial swellings are bad and somehow turn into their opposite, as, they say, nothing is drier than dropsy.

While turgidity attempts to reach beyond greatness, puerility is its direct opposite, altogether a lowly, petty, and ignoble fault. What is puerility? Clearly, it is an artificial notion overelaborated into frigidity. Writers slip into this kind of thing through a desire to be unusual, elaborate, and, above all, pleasing. They run aground on tawdriness and affectation.

In emotional passages we find a third kind of error which

[1] The quotation is from a lost play of Aeschylus. The fragment is incomplete because of the lacuna, and some of the phrases complained of do not occur in the lines as we have them. This, however, could have happened even if we had no lacuna, for Longinus often quotes only a part of a passage and expects his readers to have the whole of it in mind.

[2] This quotation from Sophocles is otherwise unknown.

borders on puerility. Theodorus [3] used to call it *parenthyrsos* or false enthusiasm. It is a display of passion, hollow and untimely, where none is needed, or immoderate where moderation is required. For writers are frequently carried away by artificial emotions of their own making which have no relation to their subject matter. Like drunkards, they are beside themselves, but their audience is not, and their passion naturally appears unseemly to those who are not moved at all. However, we shall deal with emotion elsewhere.

4

The other of the faults we mentioned—namely, frigidity—abounds in Timaeus,[1] in other respects an able writer and not without occasional greatness. Though learned and ingenious, he is, however, most critical of errors in others while unaware of his own; he is so eager always to discover strange conceits that he frequently lapses into extreme childishness. One or two things I will quote, though Caecilius has already seized upon most of them. Praising Alexander the Great, Timaeus says: "He conquered all Asia in less time than Isocrates took to write his *Panegyric* on war with Persia." This comparison of the Macedonian with the Sophist is astonishing; evidently, O Timaeus, the Spartans were far behind Isocrates in valor, since they took thirty years to conquer Messene while he marshaled his *Panegyric* in only ten! And how does he elaborate his description of the Athenians captured in Sicily? "Because of their impiety toward Hermes and the mutilation of his images, they were punished largely at the hands of one man who was a descendant of the outraged god on his father's side, Hermocrates the son of Hermon." I am surprised, my dear Terentianus, that he does not say of the tyrant Dionysius: "Because of his impiety toward Zeus and Heracles, he was deposed by Dion and Heraclides."

Why speak of Timaeus when literary giants like Xenophon and Plato, brought up in Socrates' school as they were, forget

[3] This is generally thought to be Theodorus of Gadara. See p. xx, n. 22.
[1] Timaeus of Taurumenium in Sicily.

themselves in feeble displays of wit? The former writes of the young Spartans in his *Constitution of the Lacedaemonians:* "They were less likely to speak than stone statues, bronze images were more likely to glance aside, you would think them more modest than the very pupils of their eyes." To speak of "modest pupils" is more like Amphicrates than Xenophon, as if, by Heracles, one could believe that the glances of all these men were modest, whereas impudence, as the saying goes, is betrayed especially by the eyes, and the poet says of a bold man: "Wine-bibber, with the eyes of a dog."[2]

And then Timaeus, as if he had come upon something worth stealing, does not leave this frigid phrase to Xenophon. He is talking of Agathocles who abducted his cousin and kidnaped her in the middle of her wedding: "Who would do this whose eyes had modest, not immodest pupils!"

But then the otherwise divine Plato refers to writing tablets by saying: "They shall write down these records and keep cypress-wood memorials of them in their temples." And elsewhere he says: "As for the walls, Megillus, I should agree with Sparta to let the city walls sleep in the ground and not to rouse them." The expression used by Herodotus is not much better when he says that beautiful women are "a pain to the eyes." He has, it is true, some excuse in that the speakers are barbarians and they are drunk, but even through the mouths of such characters one should not disgrace oneself before posterity by such petty expressions.[3]

---

[2] These insulting words are addressed by Achilles to Agamemnon in *Iliad* 1. 225. Xenophon's pun on the word *korê*, a maiden and the pupil of the eye, is untranslatable (*The Constitution of the Lacedaemonians* 3. 5). He replaces *korê* by *parthenos*, which also means maiden. Timaeus then goes one better by replacing it by *pornê*, which means a prostitute. We can only agree with Longinus' verdict that both passages are "frigid."

[3] The last three quotations in this chapter are Plato *Laws* 5. 741c (where he is establishing the sanctity of contracts) and 6. 778d (where he argues that walled cities may encourage cowardice in the field) and Herodotus 5. 18. 4. The criticisms of Plato seem justified, that of Herodotus seems more doubtful, but it is a question of taste and of the associations of the words actually used.

5

All such frivolities in discourse are due to the same cause, namely, a desire for novel conceits, the chief mania of our time. Good things and bad come from much the same sources. Beauties of style, great ability, and also the wish to please contribute to effective writing, yet these very things are the elements and sources of failure as well as of success. The same is true of variety, hyperbole, and the use of the poetic plural. We shall show later the risks involved in their use. At the moment we must note the problem and suggest ways of avoiding the pitfalls which beset those who attempt great writing.

6

We can do so, my friend, if we first gain some clear knowledge and critical judgment of what is truly great. This is not easy to attain, for literary judgment is the last outgrowth of long experience. Nevertheless, to speak in precepts, it is perhaps not impossible to acquire discernment in some such way as this.

7

One should realize, my friend, that, as in everyday life, nothing is noble which it is noble to despise. Wealth, honors, reputation, absolute power, and all things which are accompanied by much external and theatrical pomp—these no sensible man would count as blessings, since to despise them is in itself no mean blessing. Rather than those who possess these things, men admire those great souls who could possess them but in fact disdain them. And so it is with distinguished passages in poetry or prose; we must beware of the mere outward semblance of greatness, which is overlaid with many carelessly fashioned ornaments but on closer scrutiny proves to be hollow conceit. This it is nobler to despise than to admire.

Our soul is naturally uplifted by the truly great; we receive it as a joyous offering; we are filled with delight and pride as if we had ourselves created what we heard.

Any piece of writing which is heard repeatedly by a man of intelligence and experience yet fails to stir his soul to noble thoughts and does not leave impressed upon his mind reflections which reach beyond what was said, and which on further observation is seen to fade and be forgotten—that is not truly great writing, as it is only remembered while it is before us. The truly great can be pondered again and again; it is difficult, indeed impossible to withstand, for the memory of it is strong and hard to efface.

Consider truly great and beautiful writing to be that which satisfies all men at all times; for whenever men of different occupations, lives, interests, generations, and tongues all have one and the same opinion on the same subject, then the agreed verdict of such various elements acquires an authority so strong that the object of its admiration is beyond dispute.

8

There are, we might say, five sources most productive of great writing. All five presuppose the power of expression without which there is no good writing at all. First and most important is vigor of mental conception, which we defined in our work on Xenophon. Second is strong and inspired emotion. Both of these are for the most part innate dispositions. The others are benefited also by artistic training. They are: the adequate fashioning of figures (both of speech and of thought), nobility of diction which in turn includes the choice of words and the use of figurative and artistic language; lastly, and including all the others, dignified and distinguished word-arrangement.

Let us now investigate what is included under each heading; but first we must preface our discussion by pointing out that Caecilius omitted some things. For example, he neglects emotion. If he did so because he believed greatness and passion to be one and the same thing, so that they coincide and naturally correspond, he is mistaken. There are lowly emotions which do not go with great writing: pity, grief and fear; there are also great passages devoid of passion. Among innumerable examples we have the lines of the poet on the Aloadae: [1]

> On top of high Olympus then they strove
> To pile Mount Ossa, then again on Ossa
> Mighty Pelion with its quivering forests,
> Thus making them a stairway up to Heaven

and the even mightier words that follow:

> And this had they accomplished . . . .

The encomia, ceremonial, and display speeches of our orators are full of weighty and great passages, but they are mostly devoid of passion. Hence we find that passionate speakers rarely write encomia, while those who do write them are the least passionate.

On the other hand, if Caecilius thought that passion was not worth mentioning because it does not contribute to great writing, he was altogether deceived. For I would make bold to say that nothing contributes to greatness as much as noble passion in the right place; it breathes the frenzied spirit of its inspiration upon the words and makes them, as it were, prophetic.

9

However that may be, our first source of greatness—I mean natural high-mindedness—is the most important. It is inborn rather than acquired, but we must nevertheless educate the mind to greatness as far as possible and impregnate it, as it

---

[1] *Odyssey* 11. 315-317. "The poet" in such contexts, unless otherwise named, means *the* poet, i.e., Homer. By *pathos* (passion or strong emotion) Longinus means the expression of emotion rather than the emotional reaction of the hearer or reader, and in this sense the lines quoted have no passion though they have grandeur and might arouse wonder. It is startling to find pity, grief, and fear, especially the first and last, classed as *not* conducive to greatness, but here again Longinus seems to be thinking of passages that directly express them rather than arouse them.

were, with a noble exaltation. How? you will ask. I have written elsewhere that great writing is the echo of a noble mind. Hence the thought alone can move one to admiration even without being uttered, because of its inherent nobility. For example, the silence of Ajax in the Nekuia is superb, greater than any speech he could make.[1]

We should, then, first establish the source of this greatness, and that a true writer's mind can be neither humble nor ignoble. Men whose thoughts and concerns are mean and petty throughout life cannot produce anything admirable or worthy of lasting fame. The authors of great works are endowed with dignity of mind, and literary excellence belongs to those of high spirit.

As Alexander replied to Parmenio who said: "I would have been satisfied . . ."[2]

.   .   .   .

. . . the distance from earth to heaven.[3] One might take this to be the measure of Homer as well as of Strife. Quite unlike this is Hesiod's description of Gloom, if indeed the *Shield* too is a work of his:

Snot from her nostrils flows . . . .

[1] In *Odyssey* 11. 553-567 Odysseus meets Ajax in the underworld. It will be remembered that Ajax had committed suicide in a fit of madness after the arms of Achilles had been given to Odysseus by the Greeks. Here Odysseus asks him to forget his anger, but Ajax strides away without a word.

[2] We can complete this anecdote from Arrian's *Anabasis* 2. 25. During the siege of Tyre proposals came from Darius offering a ransom of 10,000 talents for his wife, mother, and children, all the land west of the Euphrates, and his daughter in marriage. In council Parmenio stated that, if he were Alexander, he would be satisfied to end the war on these terms. Alexander replied that he too would be satisfied to do so if he were Parmenio, but being Alexander, he would refuse.

[3] When the text is here resumed, Longinus is evidently discussing *Iliad* 4. 440-445 where Ares is rousing men to battle accompanied by Athena, Fear, Panic, and Strife, "whose head reaches to Heaven while she walks upon the Earth."

The image is not awesome but loathsome. How, on the other hand, does Homer magnify the divine?

> Far as a man can see from a high rock
> Over the wine-dark ocean's wide expanse,
> The thundering steeds of gods leap at one bound! [4]

He measures their leaps in cosmic dimensions. Would not this extravagance of grandeur make one exclaim that if the divine steeds were to leap twice in succession they would find no place to land within the universe? The imagery of the Battle of the Gods too is superlative:

> The heavens trumpeted, and high Olympus . . .

> In terror Hades, Lord of all the dead,
> Leapt screaming from his throne, for fear Poseidon,
> The god of earthquake, cleave the earth apart
> And bare his dank abode to gods and men,
> That awesome hell, loathed even by the gods. [5]

You see, my friend, how the whole earth is torn apart from its depths, the underworld itself is laid bare, and all things in heaven and hell, mortal and immortal, share the perils of this war and this battle. These things are terrifying; yet from another point of view they are, unless understood allegorically, altogether impious and transgress the boundaries of good taste.

Homer's stories of wounds, factions, revenge, tears, chains, and confused passions among the gods make the men of the Trojan War as far as possible into gods and the gods into men. Our lives of misfortune find a haven from ills in death. As for the Homeric gods, it is their miseries rather than their divine nature which are made immortal.

---

[4] The Hesiodic (?) line is from the *Shield of Heracles* (267); it is contrasted with *Iliad* 5. 770-772.

[5] The two quotations from Homer are not continuous passages. The trumpeting of heaven is in *Iliad* 21. 388, while the five following verses are 22. 61-65.

Far superior to the Battle of the Gods are those passages which represent the divine as truly pure and mighty, as in the lines on Poseidon which many critics have discussed:

> Great forests, mountains, the summits of Ida,
> The Trojan city and the Achaean fleet
> Trembled as great Poseidon strode the earth.

> Over the waves he drove, and all the beasts
> In the deep ocean, joyful, knew their lord
> And the waves gladly parted; on they flew.[6]

In this manner also the lawgiver of the Jews, no ordinary man, since he recognized and expressed divine power according to its worth, expressed that power clearly when he wrote at the beginning of his Laws: "And God said." What? "Let there be light, and there was light; let there be land, and there was land."

I trust I shall not weary you, my friend, if I compare with this one more passage from our poet, this time about humans, so that we may realize how he is wont to rise to heroic greatness. The words are spoken by Ajax who is helpless because fog and paralyzing darkness have spread over the Greeks in battle:

> Ward off this gloomy darkness, father Zeus,
> Restore the light, grant that our eyes may see,
> And in the light destroy us, if you must.[7]

How well this describes the feelings of Ajax! He does not pray for life, for that prayer were unworthy of the hero, but no display of bravery is possible in the disabling darkness and he is angry because he cannot fight. So he prays for immediate light in order that, even if Zeus is against him, he may meet a death worthy of his virtue. Here Homer blows upon

---

[6] The description of Poseidon is gathered from various places in the *Iliad*, namely 13. 18, 20. 60, 13. 19, 13. 27-29. Longinus seems to be quoting from memory.

[7] *Iliad* 17. 645-647.

the fires of battle like a directing wind, and his own feelings can be described as:

> Mad, as Ares is mad when hurling his spear,
> As is deadly fire raging on the hills
> Or in the forest deep; and from his lips
> Foam started . . . . [8]

Throughout the *Odyssey* (and there are many reasons why we must examine it also) Homer shows that storytelling is characteristic of genius in the decline of old age. There are many other indications that he composed the *Odyssey* after the *Iliad*, besides the fact that it contains many episodes of the Trojan War, remnants from the *Iliad*, and tributes of lamentation and pity which imply knowledge of deeds done long ago. The *Odyssey* may well be considered as a sequel to the *Iliad*.

> There lie Ajax the warrior, Achilles,
> Patroclus, like to the gods in council,
> And my own son beloved . . . . [9]

This, I think, is also the reason why the whole *Iliad*, written at the height of the poet's inspiration, is full of dramatic action, while the *Odyssey* is mostly narrative, which is characteristic of old age. One might compare the Homer of the *Odyssey* to the setting sun: the grandeur remains but not the intensity. The tension is not as great as in those famous lays of the *Iliad*, the great passages are not sustained without weakening, there is no such continuous outpouring of passion and suffering, no such versatility or realism or condensation of imaginative truth. It is like an ocean that has withdrawn into itself, into the solitude of its own boundaries. Greatness ebbs and flows, as the poet wanders into the mythical and the incredible. In saying this I do not forget the storm scenes of the *Odyssey*, the adventure with the Cyclops, and other things. When I speak of old age, it is the old age of Homer still, but in it all the stories are more important than the action.

[8] *Iliad* 15. 605-607.
[9] *Odyssey* 3. 109-111.

The object of this digression is, as I said, to show that genius past its prime easily turns at times to nonsense, such as the stories of the wineskin, Circe's turning men into a herd of swine (weeping piglets, as Zoïlus called them), the doves nurturing Zeus like a nestling, the ten days without food after shipwreck, and the unconvincing slaughter of the suitors. What else can we call these stories, in truth, but the dreaming of a Zeus? Another reason for discussing the *Odyssey* is that you may realize that the declining passion of great writers of prose and poetry is apt to relax into character stories, such as the sketches of life in the house of Odysseus. Such descriptions of ordinary life are more like a comedy of manners.[10]

10 The difference between the *Iliad* and the *Odyssey*, in one of its aspects, is here expressed as the difference between the two Greek words *pathos* and *êthos*. Aristotle makes a similar statement in the *Poetics* (24. 2; 1459b. 14-16). The meaning of *pathos* is quite clear: it refers to any passion or strong emotion (in the *Poetics* there may also be a reference to the sense "suffering") and the word thus very naturally became associated with violent appeals to emotions which are characteristic of the grand manner or style. No one would deny that the *Iliad* contains more passion and tragedy than the *Odyssey*. The word *êthos*, however, is more complicated. In criticism it naturally refers to characterization and to speaking in character, but it is surprising to find both Aristotle and Longinus telling us that characterization is better in the *Odyssey*, as this is simply not the case. That is in fact not their meaning. The writer who is good at speaking "in character" is one who is distinguished by his *naturalness*, and this was especially true of the orator Lysias. It is also true that, as contrasted with the heroic tone of tragedy, comedy represents life at a lower level, a more natural, lifelike level. So the word *êthos* comes to be associated with comedy and, in prose, with a more natural, less exalted style, and *pathos* with tragedy and the grand manner. This is the meaning here: the *Iliad* is more passionate, tragic, elevated, the *Odyssey* more natural, lifelike, simple. This development of the word is quite early, since we find it so used in the *Poetics*. There is an interesting discussion of *pathos* and *êthos* in Quintilian (6. 2. 4-24), who tells us that *êthos* often refers to milder emotions which require a less exalted style, and a briefer contrast in Cicero (*Orator* 37. 128). Some interesting illustrations of the various meanings of *êthos* will be found in an article by J. F. Lockwood in *Classical Quarterly* 23 (1929), 180-185.

10

Let us consider now whether we can point to any other factor which can make writing great. There are, in every situation, a number of features which combine to make up the texture of events. To select the most vital of these and to relate them to one another to form a unified whole is an essential cause of great writing. One writer charms the reader by the selection of such details, another by the manner in which he presses them into close relationship.

Sappho, for example, selects on each occasion the emotions which accompany the frenzy of love. She takes these from among the constituent elements of the situation in actual life. How does she excel? In her skillful choice of the most important and intense details and in relating them to one another:

> Peer of gods he seemeth to me, the blissful
> Man who sits and gazes at thee before him,
> Close beside thee sits, and in silence hears thee
> Silvery speaking,
>
> Laughing Love's low laughter. Oh this, this only
> Stirs the troubled heart in my breast to tremble,
> For should I but see thee a little moment,
> Straight is my voice hushed;
>
> Yea, my tongue is broken, and through and through me
> 'Neath the flesh, impalpable fire runs tingling;
> Nothing see mine eyes, and a noise of roaring
> Waves in my ears sounds;
>
> Sweat runs down in rivers, a tremor seizes
> All my limbs and paler than grass in autumn,
> Caught by pains of menacing death, I falter,
> Lost in the love trance.[1]

1 This famous ode of Sappho of Lesbos (early sixth century B.C.) is preserved only here. The translation is that of J. A. Symonds (1883); it keeps something of the Sapphic meter. At the end of the poem the first line of another stanza is preserved in our texts which translators naturally ignore, for the poem there breaks off, and it makes little sense ("all must be dared since one who is poor . . ."). This is the ode imitated by Catullus (51).

Do you not marvel how she seeks to make her mind, body, ears, tongue, eyes, and complexion, as if they were scattered elements strange to her, join together in the same moment of experience? In contradictory phrases she describes herself as hot and cold at once, rational and irrational, at the same time terrified and almost dead, in order to appear afflicted not by one passion but by a swarm of passions. Lovers do have all those feelings, but it is, as I said, her selection of the most vital details and her working them into one whole which produce the outstanding quality of the poem.

In the same way, as I believe, Homer picks out what is hardest to endure when describing a storm. The author of the *Arimaspeia*,[2] on the other hand, thinks this awe-inspiring:

> It is a marvel to us, to our minds,
> That men should dwell at sea, so far from land.
> Unfortunate creatures, many ills are theirs,
> Their eyes fixed on the sky, their minds on the deep.
> Often to heaven they raise up their hands
> In a sad prayer from their heaving hearts.

Everyone can plainly see that there is here more froth than terror. How does Homer do it? Here is an example among many:

> He rushed upon them, as a wave storm-driven,
> Boisterous beneath black clouds, on a swift ship
> Will burst, and all is hidden in the foam;
> Meanwhile the wind tears thundering at the mast,
> And all hands tremble, pale and sore afraid,
> As they are carried close from under death.[3]

Aratus tried to adapt the same idea:

> Thin planks keep death away.[4]

He has made his description trivial and smooth instead of terrifying. Indeed, he has circumscribed the danger in the words "planks keep death away," for in fact they do keep it

2 Said by Herodotus (4. 13-15) to be one Aristeas of Proconnesus, about 600 B.C.

3 The Homeric passage is a simile, *Iliad* 15. 624-628.

4 *Phainomena* 287.

away! Homer does not limit the danger to one moment; instead, he draws a picture of men avoiding destruction many times, at every wave; he forces and compels into unnatural union prepositions which are not easily joined together when he says "*from under* death." He has tortured his line into conformity with the impending disaster, and by the compactness of his language he brilliantly represents the calamity and almost stamps upon the words the very shape of the peril: "they are carried from under death." The same is true of Archilochus' description of a shipwreck and of Demosthenes' description of news of defeat reaching Athens in the passage which begins: "It was evening . . ." [5]

These writers have sifted out the most significant details on the basis of merit, so to speak, and joined them harmoniously without inserting between them anything irrelevant, frivolous, or artificial; such additions spoil the total effect just as the imperfect adjustment of massive stones that are fitted together into a wall spoils the whole structure if chinks and fissures are left between them.

11

The quality called amplification is akin to those we have already discussed. It occurs wherever circumstances of the case admit many pauses and fresh starts from time to time and fine, well-rounded passages succeed one another, increasing the effect at every step. Amplification consists of the development of commonplaces, emotional intensification, emphasis on facts, stylistic elaborations, the rearrangement of subject matter, or emotional appeals. There are innumerable kinds of amplification, but the speaker should realize that not one of them is completely effective when divorced from greatness, except perhaps in appeals to pity or attempts to disparage.

All other kinds of amplification, if divorced from greatness, are like a body without a soul and become slack and hollow.

[5] *On the Crown* 169, describing how news of the capture of Elatea was received in Athens.

And since the selection of vital details and their arrangement into a unified whole, which we discussed above, also constitute a kind of elaboration, we should, for the sake of clarity, explain where the difference lies, and also that between amplification and greatness.

12

I am not satisfied with the definition of amplification given in the textbooks. They say that amplification is a manner of expression which enhances the subject. This might equally well be a definition of greatness or of passion or of figurative language, for all these enhance the subject in some way, but they differ from one another. Greatness implies distinction, amplification implies quantity; the former can exist in a single thought, the latter always involves length and a certain abundance. In general terms, amplification means expatiating upon the various aspects and topics involved in a situation; it strengthens and elaborates a description by dwelling upon it. It differs in this way from proof because the latter demonstrates a point . . .

. . . opulently, like a sea, it often spreads into wide open grandeur. The orator, being more passionate, has, as might be expected, much fire and flaming spirit. The other, secure in his dignity and proud magnificence, while not frigid, is not as compact.[1]

In much the same way, my dear Terentianus, Cicero and Demosthenes differ in their great passages—in so far as a Greek like myself can be allowed to judge.[2] Demosthenes' greatness

1 We cannot be sure which two writers are being compared, but what is said of "the orator" fits Demosthenes very well, and the other is probably Plato, for we are said to "return to him" at the beginning of ch. 13.

2 This modesty may be quite sincere. Greek critics practically never discuss Latin writers, but the Romans do not hesitate to discuss the Greeks. This is not merely discretion toward the masters of the world; there are several good reasons for it. The Greeks did not need to refer to Roman

is usually more abrupt; he is always forceful, rapid, powerful, and intense; he may be compared to the lightning or the thunderbolt which burns and ravages. Cicero, to me, is like an enveloping conflagration which spreads all around and crowds upon us, a vast steady fire which flares up in this direction or that and is fed intermittently. You Romans would be better judges of this, but the tense greatness of Demosthenes is more suited to moments of intense and violent passion when the audience must be altogether swept off its feet. The right time for the Ciceronian copiousness is when the audience must be overwhelmed by a flood of words; it is appropriate when elaborating a commonplace, in perorations for the most part, in digressions, descriptions, and display speeches, in works of history and natural science as well as on many other occasions.

13

You have read the *Republic* and you know that Plato's writing (to return to him) flows in a smooth and copious stream, yet achieves greatness. You remember his manner:

> The inexperienced in wisdom and virtue, ever occupied with feasting and such, are carried downward, and there, as is fitting, they wander their whole life long, neither ever looking upward to the truth above them nor rising toward it, nor tasting pure and lasting pleasures. Like cattle, always looking downward with their heads bent toward the ground and the banquet tables, they feed, fatten, and fornicate. In order to increase their possessions they kick and butt with horns and hoofs of steel and kill each other, insatiable as they are.[1]

---

literature, whereas the Romans could not ignore the Greek writers whom they had always taken as their models. Moreover, the educated Romans of the empire were practically bilingual, so that they had a right to judge the Greeks, whereas very few Greeks knew Latin well. We know that Caecilius had written a comparative criticism of Demosthenes and Cicero, for he is taken to task by Plutarch, a century later, for having done so (*Life of Demosthenes* 3). It is probably this work which Longinus has in mind here.

[1] *Republic* 9. 586a-b.

Plato shows us, if we are willing to listen, that there is another road to greatness besides those already mentioned. What is this road? It is the emulation and imitation of the great prose writers and poets of the past. This, my dear friend, is an aim we should never abandon. Many a man derives inspiration from another spirit in the same way as the Pythian priestess at Delphi, when she approaches the tripod at the place where there is a cleft in the ground, is said to inhale a divine vapor; thus at once she becomes impregnated with divine power and, suddenly inspired, she utters oracles. So from the genius of the ancients exhalations flow, as from the sacred clefts, into the minds of those who emulate them, and even those little inclined to inspiration become possessed by the greatness of others.

Was it only Herodotus who was very Homeric? There were Stesichorus and Archilochus before him, and then Plato, more than any other writer, draws many channels from that great Homeric river into his own work. We might have had to prove this, if Ammonius [2] and his school had not classified and recorded his debts in detail. This is not stealing; it is like modeling oneself upon beautiful characters, images, or works of art. Plato would not, I think, have reached the same heights in his philosophical expositions, nor so frequently have ventured upon poetic matter or style, if he had not, like a young antagonist breaking a lance with an established champion, eagerly contended with Homer for the first place, overambitiously perhaps, but certainly not without profit. In the words of Hesiod,[3] this kind of strife is a blessing to men. And in truth this is a beautiful and worthy contest, in which even defeat by one's predecessors is not without glory.

2 Probably the pupil of Aristarchus (second century B.C.).

3 *Works and Days* 11-24, where a contrast is drawn between two kinds of Eris or Strife; the first leads to war and conflict, the second (emulation) is a blessing for men.

14

And it is right for us, too, whenever we are laboring over a piece of writing which requires greatness in thought or expression, to imagine how Homer might perchance have said it, how Plato, or Demosthenes, or in history Thucydides, would have made it great. For as we emulate them, these eminent personages are present in our minds and raise us to a higher level of imaginative power. The more so if we add the thought: "How would these words of mine strike Homer or Demosthenes? What would they think of them?" It is indeed a trial to submit our work to such a jury and to such an audience, and to imagine, if only in play, that we have to give an account of our literary stewardship to these giants as our judges and witnesses.

An even greater incentive is to ask the question: how will posterity receive what I write? For if a man is actually afraid to utter anything that looks beyond his own life and time, then his mind's conceptions are destined to be imperfect and blind; they will miscarry, nor ever grow into the perfection which deserves later fame.

15

Besides this, my young friend, a most effective way of attaining weight, dignity, and realism [1] is provided by the imagination. Some call it image-making. In the general sense, any thought present in the mind and producing speech is called imagination, but in its now prevailing sense the word applies when ecstasy or passion makes you appear to see what you

[1] The Greek word *agon* means contest and refers to an actual case in court, sometimes a real political struggle and the like. Cicero and Quintilian frequently speak of the "real battles" of the courts as requiring more vigor in style, etc., as against works merely published. So the Greek word *agon* and its derivatives come to mean actuality or realism, and this is a closer translation than "power" or "vividness," which are specific qualities and have other specific names.

are describing and enables you to make your audience see it.
You will be aware that imagination has a different aim in
oratory than in poetry. The poet seeks to enthrall, the orator
aims at vividness. Both, however, attempt to excite their
audience.

> Mother, I beg you, do not set on me
> The snaky Furies with their bleeding eyes.
> Closer and closer they are rushing at me . . .

and:

> Alas! She slays me. Whither shall I flee? [2]

Here the poet himself sees the Furies, and very nearly compels
his audience to see what he has imagined. Euripides spares
no pains in wringing tragic effects from the two passions of
madness and love and he is probably more successful in this
than in anything else, though he is bold enough in other
kinds of imaginative effort. He had little natural genius, yet he
forced such talent as he had to rise to tragedy very often, and
in all his great passages, like Homer's wounded lion,

> He lashes with his tail his ribs and flank
> And goads himself to battle . . . .[3]

For example, when Helios hands the reins to Phaethon, he
says:

> "Invade not on your course the Libyan sky;
> It has no moisture, and its burning heat
> Will scorch your chariot wheels . . . ."

Then he goes on:

2 The two quotations are from Euripides, the first *Orestes* 255-257, the
second *Iphigenia in Tauris* 291. The general verdict of the ancient critics
on Euripides was that he was less poetic (either in diction or natural
talent) than Sophocles, but a master in tragic effects and dramatization of
passion. He was also, of course, regarded as a more useful model for orators. Cf. what is said of him in ch. 40 and, in particular, in Aristotle,
Poetics 13.6 (1453a 29) and 18.7 (1456a 25), *Rhetoric* 3.2.5; Dionysius of
Halicarnassus, *On Ancient Writers* 2.11; and Quintilian 2.1.67-68.

3 *Iliad* 20.170-171.

"Hold on your course toward the Pleiades."
The youth, when he thus ended, snatched the reins;
He lashed the winged team, the bridle loosed.
They flew into the valleys of the sky.
Astride the Sirian star the father followed
Wisely advising: "Drive this way. Here turn
Your chariot . . . ." [4]

Would you not think that the poet's mind itself travels along in the chariot and shares the perils of that winged team's flight? If it had not followed them on their heavenly journey, he could not have thus depicted it. The words of his Cassandra are of the same kind: "Nay, horse-loving Trojans . . . ." [5]

Aeschylus is daring in his flights of heroic imagination. He says of the Seven against Thebes:

The seven captains, leaders of the host,
Slaughtered a bull over a black-rimmed shield;
Steeping their hands in the bull's flowing gore
They swore by Ares, Enyo, bloody Panic . . . [6]

swearing an oath of mutual loyalty unto death, pitilessly. But at times Aeschylus' conceptions are harsh, left in the rough, as it were, uncarded. Even Euripides, when he tries to compete with him, runs this risk. Aeschylus, in describing the Epiphany of Dionysus, paradoxically says that the palace of Lycurgus is inspired:

The halls possessed, the roof in Bacchic frenzy,

whereas Euripides expresses the same thought by a different and more pleasing phrase:

Then the whole mountain joined in Bacchic frenzy. [7]

Sophocles displays supreme imaginative power when describing Oedipus preparing his own burial amidst divine portents,

---

[4] The two quotations are from a lost play of Euripides, the *Phaethon*.

[5] The half-line spoken by Cassandra is from another lost play of Euripides, the *Alexander*.

[6] *Seven Against Thebes* 42-46.

[7] The first quotation is from a lost play of Aeschylus, and the verse compared with it favorably is Euripides, *Bacchants* 726.

or Achilles appearing above his tomb before the departing Greeks, though I doubt if anyone has represented this last scene more vividly than Simonides.[8] However, we cannot quote all such passages.

Poetic imagination, as already mentioned, admits the more fabulous and incredible, whereas the best feature of the orator's images is actuality and probability. When this rule is broken, when a prose image is poetical and fabulous and altogether impossible, the result is weird and precarious, as when our clever orators see Furies, as tragic poets do, and the noble fellows cannot realize the simple fact that when Orestes says

> Unhand me, you who midst my band of Furies,
> Gripping me fast to hurl me down to Hell . . .[9]

he sees the Furies because he is mad! What then is the function of oratorical imagination? Perhaps to contribute vigor and passion also in other ways, but, above all, when mingled with practical argumentation, to master the hearer rather than persuade him, as in this passage of Demosthenes:

> If at this moment loud shouting were heard outside the courthouse and we were told that the gates of the prison are open and the prisoners escaping, no man, young or old, is so indifferent that he would not give all the help he can. And if someone then came to tell us that this is the man who let them out, he would be killed at once, before he had a chance to speak . . . .[10]

Hyperides does the same. He had been brought to trial because of his proposal, after the defeat of Athens, to free the slaves. He said: "It was not I, the speaker, who framed this bill, but the battle of Chaeroneia."[11] In the midst of prac-

---

8 The Oedipus scene is from *Oedipus at Colonus* 1586-1645, and the appearance of Achilles from a lost play of Sophocles. Simonides (*c.* 556-468 B.C.) was a very famous writer of lyric and elegiac verse.

9 Euripides, *Orestes* 264-265.

10 *Against Timocrates* 208.

11 For this incident see Plutarch *Moralia* 848d-850b.

tical arguments he uses his imagination, and thus goes beyond persuasion. In all such cases the more dynamic phrase catches our ear; our attention is drawn away from the argument's proof and we are startled by an imaginative picture which conceals the actual argument by its own brilliance. This is natural enough; when two things are joined into one, the stronger diverts to itself the power of the weaker.

This will be enough about greatness derived from ideas and due to nobility of mind, emulation, or imagination.

16

This is the place to deal with figures. These also, as I mentioned, contribute materially to greatness if they are rightly handled. However, a detailed exposition of all the figures is too great a task on this occasion—indeed, it would be an endless task. I shall therefore deal only with a few of those which complement greatness in order to prove my point.

Demosthenes is trying to vindicate his policies.[1] What would have been the natural way of speaking? "You were not wrong to take up the fight for the liberty of Greece. You have precedents for this, as they were not wrong who fought at Marathon, at Salamis, or at Plataea." But when, like a man suddenly inspired and, as it were, god-possessed, he utters that oath by the heroes of Greece: "It cannot be that you were wrong, by those who faced death at Marathon . . . ," through the use of that one figure, the oath (though here I should call it an *apostrophe*), he seemingly deifies their ancestors by suggesting that one may invoke those who died such a death as if they were gods; he recalls to the jury their pride in those

---

[1] As this passage of Demosthenes is discussed at such length, I append a translation of it (*On the Crown* 208):

It cannot be, it cannot be that you were wrong, men of Athens, in taking up the struggle on behalf of the liberty and safety of all. No!— by those of your ancestors who faced danger at Marathon, by those who stood in the ranks at Plataea, those who fought from their ships at Salamis and Artemisium, and many other brave men who lie in our public graves, all of whom the city deemed worthy of the same honor of public burial, Aeschines. and not only those who won and were victorious.

who faced death at Marathon; he turns what is essentially an
argument into a supremely great and passionate passage by
the appeal of this strange, extraordinary oath; he impresses
it, like some paean or charm, upon the minds of his hearers,
who are led by his praise to think with relief that they may
take as much pride in their battle against Philip as in the
victories of Marathon and Salamis. In all these ways the orator, by the use of this figure, grips his audience and carries it
along with him.

It is said that the germ of this oath is found in a comedy
of Eupolis:

> No! by Marathon, for I fought there too,
> No one shall hurt me and be glad of it.

But it is not the fact of an oath that is important, but the
place, the manner, the occasion, and the purpose. In Eupolis
it is only an oath, addressed to an Athens still prosperous and
in no need of consolation; it does not immortalize the men
in order to rouse the audience to thoughts worthy of their
courage, but the poet's attention wanders away from the men
who face danger to the inanimate abstraction, the battle. In
Demosthenes, the oath is carefully phrased and addressed to
men who had been defeated, so that the Athenians should no
longer consider Chaeroneia as a failure. And so this one
figure is at the same time a proof that their action had not
been wrong, a precedent, the confirmation of an oath, an encomium, and an exhortation.

Then, to counter his opponent's objection: "The policy you
speak of led to defeat, and you swear by victories," he carefully weighs every word and uses those not open to this objection, thus showing us that even in a moment of frenzied
passion sobriety is essential. He speaks of "those who faced
danger at Marathon, those who fought in ships at Salamis
and Artemisium, those who stood in the ranks at Plataea." He
does not use the word "victorious" anywhere; he avoids any
word that would indicate the successful outcome which was
the opposite of Chaeroneia. That is also why he forestalls

this thought in his hearers' minds by adding at once: "And the city gave a public funeral to them all, Aeschines, not only to the victorious."

17

We should not here omit, dear friend, though we shall deal with it very briefly, a subject we have studied, namely, that figures naturally reinforce greatness and are wonderfully supported by it in turn. I shall explain why and how this happens. The cunning use of figures arouses a peculiar suspicion in the hearer's mind, a feeling of being deliberately trapped and misled. This occurs when we are addressing a single judge with power of decision, and especially a dictator, a king, or an eminent leader. He is easily angered by the thought that he is being outwitted like a silly child by the expert speaker's pretty figures; he sees in the fallacious reasoning a personal insult; sometimes he may altogether give way to savage exasperation, but even if he controls his anger he remains impervious to persuasion.

That is why the best use of a figure is when the very fact that it is a figure goes unnoticed. Now greatness and passion are a wonderful help and protection against the suspicions aroused by the use of figures; cunning techniques, when overlaid with beauty and passion, disappear from view and escape all further suspicion. The oath "by those at Marathon," quoted above, is a sufficient proof of this. How has the orator there concealed the figure? Clearly, by its very brilliance. Just as dimmer lights are lost in the surrounding sunshine, so pervading grandeur all around obscures the presence of rhetorical devices. Something not very different happens in painting: light and shade are represented by colors on the same plane, yet the light is seen first, it not only stands out but seems much nearer. In the same way, great and passionate expressions affect our minds more closely; by a kind of natural kinship and brilliance they are seen before the figures, whose artistry they overshadow and keep hidden.

18

What of those well-known figures, rhetorical questions and inquiries? Does not their very form make what is said more actual and more vehement?

> Tell me, do you want to go round and inquire from one another: what is the news? What could be greater news than that a Macedonian is conquering Greece? Is Philip dead? By heavens no, but he is ill. What difference does that make to you? If something did happen to him, you would soon create another Philip.

And again he says:

> Let us sail to Macedonia. "Where shall we land?" someone asks. The war itself will reveal the weak spots in Philip's position.[1]

Simply stated, the content is quite inadequate, but the inspired, rapid turn of question and answer, the reply to himself as if he were someone else, not only make the passage more successful because the figure is used, but actually more convincing.

Passionate language is more moving when it seems to arise spontaneously and not to be contrived by the speaker, and the rhetorical question answered by oneself simulates this emotional spontaneity. For, just as when we are suddenly asked a question we are provoked to give a vigorous and truthful reply, so the figure of question and answer leads and beguiles the hearer to believe that each point has arisen and been answered spontaneously.

We should add, for it is considered to be one of the greatest passages in Herodotus . . .

.   .   .   .

[1] Demosthenes, *First Philippic* 10-11 and 44 (the second quotation is condensed).

19

. . . and the words burst forth without connectives, pour out, as it were, and the speaker himself cannot keep up with them. "Shield on shield"—says Xenophon—"they were pushing, fighting, killing, dying." [1] And the words of Eurylochus to Odysseus:

> As you had ordered, through the wood we went,
> We noticed in the glens a well-built house.[2]

The clauses are disconnected as well as hurried; they give an impression of actuality; they stop the reader and yet press on. And the poet has achieved this effect by means of asyndeton.[3]

20

A combination of figures can also be very moving when two or three are mingled together and jointly contribute to the power, persuasiveness, and beauty of a passage. In the speech against Midias, for example, we find asyndeta interwoven with anaphora or repetition and *diatyposis* or vivid representation: [1]

[1] *Hellenica* 4. 3. 19.

[2] *Odyssey* 10. 251-252.

[3] Asyndeton is much more striking in Greek, where the logical connection between clauses and sentences was regularly expressed by connective particles, whereas we are apt just to set down sentences side by side and leave the reader to grasp the connection of thought for himself.

[1] For asyndeton see ch. 19, n. 3. Anaphora is the repetition of words at the beginning of succeeding clauses. *Diatyposis* is the same figure as hypotyposis, which Quintilian calls (9. 2. 40 ff.) *sub oculos subiectio*, i.e., bringing the event you are narrating before the very eyes of your hearers, making them "see" it happen. It is doubtful whether this is properly called a figure, for it is hard to distinguish from vividness, which was discussed in ch. 15 above. See also Quintilian 8. 3. 61 ff.

The passage here discussed is from Demosthenes' speech *Against Midias* (72). The quotation is not quite exact; e.g., the words "like a slave" do not

An assailant can do many things to his victim, only a few
of which the latter can tell to anyone else—by his posture,
by his look, by his voice. . . .

Then, lest his speech should seem to mark time as it con-
tinues to deal with the same topic (for the effect of marking
time is peaceful, while in disorder there is passion which is
movement and excitement of mind), the orator rushes on to
other asyndeta and repetitions:

. . . by his posture, by his look, by his voice, now insulting,
now as an enemy, now striking with his knuckles, now
beating him like a slave.

He thus achieves the same result as the assailant, he startles
the mind of the jury by a swift succession of phrases. At this
point he starts a fresh attack, like gusts of a hurricane:

Now with his knuckles, now at his temples—he says—These
things stir men up, these things make them lose control, being unaccustomed to abuse. No one, by telling of it, can
communicate the dreadful reality.

He carefully preserves the essential force of his asyndeta and
repetitions by varying them continually. In this way the order
of his words is disorderly, but on the other hand there is a
kind of order in this disorder.

21

Come now, add the connectives if you will, after the manner
of Isocrates and his school: "Furthermore, we must not omit
the fact that an assailant could do many things, first by his
posture, then by his look, and then again by his voice . . . ."
As you expand the passage in this way point by point, and
make it smooth by adding the connectives, you will soon
realize that its urgent, rugged passion is falling flat, that its

occur in the text of Demosthenes, nor are they repeated in the third ex-
tract. There are other slight discrepancies which would seem to indicate
that our author is quoting from memory. The main point of the passage
is that the indignity of the assault is often the worst feature of it.

sting and its fire have vanished. Just as a runner is deprived of his speed when his legs are tied together, so passionate emotion resents being fettered by conjunctions and other additions, for its free course is impeded and its catapult-like impetus is lost.

22

Hyperbaton belongs to the same class of figures. It is an arrangement of words or ideas which departs from the normal sequence, and it is, as it were, the true stamp of living passion. In real life men who are angry, frightened, resentful, under the influence of jealousy or the like (for emotions are numerous, indeed innumerable, and no one can say how many there are) always jump from one subject to another, mention one thing and then often rush to something else, throw some irrelevant statement in between, and then come round again to their starting point, as their vehemence, like a changing wind, drives them in every direction. They are ever ready to wrench their words and thoughts from their natural sequence and to change that sequence in innumerable ways. The best writers imitate this aspect of real life by means of hyperbata. For art at its best is mistaken for nature, and nature is successful when it contains hidden art.

Dionysius of Phocaea says in Herodotus:

> Our fortunes are on the razor's edge, men of Ionia, whether to be free men or slaves, and runaway slaves at that. If you are willing to endure hardships now, you will face immediate difficulties, but you will be able to overcome your enemies.[1]

The natural order was: "Men of Ionia, now is the time to face hardship, for our fortunes are on the razor's edge." The speaker displaces the words "men of Ionia" and starts immediately to express his fears as if there was no time to address them first in view of the peril that besets them. Then he inverts the sequence of his thoughts. Before saying they must

[1] Herodotus 6. 11. 2.

endure hardship, which is the object of his exhortation, he first gives them the reason why they must do so by saying: "Our fortunes are on the razor's edge." His words seem forced upon him by the situation rather than premeditated.

Thucydides is particularly skillful in his use of hyperbata to separate things which are naturally one and inseparable. Demosthenes is not so arbitrary, but he is the most insatiable user of this kind of figure. By means of it he gives a strong impression of actuality and, indeed, even of speaking impromptu. Besides this, he involves his audience with him in the perilous vagaries of his prolonged hyberbata. The idea from which he started is often left in suspense; meanwhile he piles up extraneous matter in the middle of his sentence in an ostensibly strange and improbable order; he throws his audience into a panic lest his whole argument collapse as his realistic vehemence compels them to experience that danger with him; then, unexpectedly and after a long interval, he comes to the long-awaited conclusion at the end and at the right moment. By the very hazardousness and precariousness of his hyperbata he greatly increases his emotional effects. There are so many examples of this that quotation is unnecessary.

23

The figures called polyptoton, *athroïsmos, metabolé,* and climax [1]—all, as you know, give an impression of actuality and

---

[1] These figures are not explained or illustrated here, but we know their meaning from other sources:

Polyptoton is defined by Quintilian (9. 3. 87) as the use of the same word in different cases, and he gives a clear example: *pater hic tuus? patrem nunc appellas? patris tui filius es?* He carefully distinguishes it from another figure which piles up a number of different details.

Athroïsmos is defined by Quintilian (8. 4. 26-27) as the accumulation of words and sentences which have the same meaning. He calls this, in Latin, *congeries,* and carefully distinguishes it from *synathroismus,* but defines it in the same way as *metabolé* in 9. 3. 37, referred to below.

Metabolé is precisely the name which Quintilian gives to this third figure and he says it is Caecilius who gave it that name. As the word is

contribute to ornamentation, greatness, and emotional appeal.
What of changes in case, tense, person, number, and gender?
How do they diversify and enliven our utterances? As regards
number, not only are those expressions ornamental which,
though formally singular, are found, when examined, to be
plural in sense, as in

> And scattered on the beach the multitude
> Cried "tunny" . . . ,

but the reverse figure deserves fuller examination, for there
are occasions when the plural is more striking, more grand,
and more impressive because of the sense of multitude given
by the number, as:

> Marriages accursed,
> That gave us birth and, having borne us, gave
> The same seed in return, that since have made
> Fathers and sons and brothers all in one,
> Incestuous brood of mothers, wives, and brides,
> A deed most shameful among all mankind.[2]

All this spells one name only: Oedipus, and Iocasta on the
other side, yet by diffusing it into a plural the misfortunes
too are multiplied. So with the line:

> The Hectors, the Sarpedons then came out,

and Plato's description of the Athenians which we have
quoted elsewhere:

---

clearly used by Longinus to refer to a specific figure, and not in its general sense of change or variation, this is most probably the sense here.
We may note, however, that in Demetrius, *On Style* 148 it is the name of
another figure: he calls *metabolé* the immediate qualification of a statement just made, a kind of self-correction.

Climax or ladder, which Quintilian (9. 3. 56) calls *gradatio*, consists of a
series of steps, each of which is repeated before going on to the next, i.e.,
a b b c c d etc. The most famous example occurs in Demosthenes' *On
the Crown* (179): "I did not say this and not propose an embassy, I did
not propose an embassy and not go to Thebes, I did not go to Thebes
and not persuade the Thebans, but I carried the matter through from
beginning to end. . . ."

2 Sophocles, *Oedipus King* 1403-1408.

No Pelopses dwell with us or Cadmuses, no Egyptians or Danaäns or any others of the many born barbarians, but we who live here are pure Greeks, not half barbarians . . . [3]

and so on. Such a collection of names in a mass makes the subject sound more imposing. However, we must not use this figure indiscriminately, but only where the subject matter allows amplification, multiplication, hyperbole, or strong emotion, one or more of them. To go everywhere with a crier's bell is to act too much like a Sophist.

24

Then again, the opposite figure, which gathers a plurality of things under a singular noun, sometimes achieves a clearer impression of greatness, as for example: "The whole Peloponnesus was at odds . . . ," or in the sentence of Herodotus: "When Phrynichus produced his play, *The Capture of Miletus*, the whole theater burst into tears." [1]

Thus to gather separate things together and to designate them by a singular noun makes them more like one body. The reason why this is an ornament is, I think, the same in both cases. Where the singular is more normal, the unexpected use of the plural suits emotional passages; where the plural is normal, and a number of things are summed up in one fine-sounding noun, this contrary change has the effect of surprise.

[3] The passage from Plato is *Menexenus* 245d. The other two quotations in this chapter are unknown.

[1] The first example is from Demosthenes, *On the Crown* 18. The figure consists, of course, in speaking of "The Peloponnesus" instead of "the Peloponnesians." The second example is Herodotus 6. 21. 2. (The Greek text is defective here for it actually says "the spectators," which would be no figure at all, but we can confidently correct it from our text of Herodotus who does say "the theater.") It is worth noting that the effect is more striking in Greek, because they used abstract and collective nouns much less freely. For us the figure has lost all its freshness.

25

Whenever you introduce past events as happening in the present, you will be describing them as actually happening rather than narrating what has happened. Xenophon writes:

A man who has fallen under Cyrus' horse and is being trampled strikes at the animal's belly with his dagger. The horse rears and throws Cyrus. He falls.[1]

Thucydides writes in this way as often as anyone.

26

A change of person is equally realistic. It often makes the reader feel himself in the midst of the dangers described:

Fatigue you'd say they knew not, nor exhaustion,
So eagerly they battled face to face.

Or in Aratus:

Venture not on the sea during this month.

So, too, Herodotus writes:

From Elephantine you will sail up the coast, and you will then reach a flat plain. You will cross this, then embark again for a two-day voyage which will bring you to a large city called Meroe.

Do you see, my friend, how he gets a hold on your mind and leads it through these places and makes you *see* what you only hear? Such passages, by addressing the reader directly, place him in the middle of the action. There is also a less general kind of address which seems to be directed to a particular person:

On which side Diomede fought you could not tell.

By thus directly addressing your reader you will enlist his

[1] *Education of Cyrus* 7.1.37. The figure described here is the use of the historic present.

feelings more effectively, secure his attention, and make the situation completely real to him.[1]

27

Sometimes, when telling the story of one of his characters, a writer will suddenly himself speak in the person of that character. This kind of figure expresses an outburst of strong emotion:

> And Hector to the Trojans called aloud
> To rush the ships, let lie the bloody spoils,
> "If I see one of his own will hold back,
> I shall see to it that he dies . . . ."

The poet tells the story, as is fitting, in his own person; but the sudden threat is abruptly, without warning, spoken in the person of the angry leader. The passionate tone would be lowered if he added: "And Hector said—this and that." The change of person has suddenly outpaced the writer who makes it. This figure should be used when a sharp crisis does not allow the writer to delay, and compels a change of person. We find this also in Hecataeus:

> Ceyx thought this a dreadful thing, and at once ordered the Heraclidae to depart: "I cannot help you. To avoid perishing yourselves and injuring me, go to another country."

Demosthenes uses the change of person in a somewhat different way in his speech against Aristogeiton to express a swift turn of passion:

> Shall we not find one among you angry or indignant at the violence of this vulgar, shameless fellow who—you foulest of men, when license of speech was forbidden you not by any bar or gate that might be opened . . . .

Before the thought is completed he breaks off; in his anger he almost splits one phrase into pieces by using the third and

[1] The references in this chapter are *Iliad* 15. 697-698; Aratus *Phainomena* 299; Herodotus 2. 29. 2-6 (very much from memory and not at all exact); *Iliad* 5. 85. This use of the second person is also much more vivid and fresh in Greek.

second person simultaneously: "who—you foulest . . ."; and so when his speech seems to have turned away from Aristogeiton and left him, his passion concentrates on him even more.

The words of Penelope are very similar:

> Herald, why have these high-born suitors sent you?
> Is it to tell the maids of great Odysseus
> To leave their work, prepare for them a feast?
> Would this were now their last repast of all,
> That they might never come or woo again—
> You who devour so freely all our substance,
> Have you not ever listened to your fathers
> When you were children and you heard them tell
> What kind of man Odysseus was. . . .[1]

28

No one will doubt, I think, that a periphrasis can contribute to greatness. Just as in music so-called variations add charm and perfection to the principal theme, so the periphrasis is often in tune with the plain statement and greatly embellishes it, especially if it contains nothing swollen or discordant and is pleasantly composed. Plato's words at the beginning of the funeral speech are sufficient proof of this:

> Our action has given these men our fitting tribute; having received it, they proceed on their fated journey, accom-

[1] Four examples are given in this chapter, the first and last from Homer (*Iliad* 15. 346-349 and *Odyssey* 4. 681-689); the second from Hecataeus of Miletus, a historian and geographer of the sixth century B.C. whose works are lost; the third from Demosthenes (*Against Aristogeiton* 1. 27-28). Longinus takes all four as illustrating "change of person," and this is technically correct, but he is dealing with two essentially different figures. In the first two examples the verb of saying is omitted and the writer suddenly drops into direct speech without transition. This is abrupt, but not startling, nor indeed very unusual. The last two examples are much more violent: here the speaker, in the middle of the speech, suddenly addresses the character of whom he is talking. This is much more passionate and causes a break in the syntax. It is really a form of apostrophe (see Quintilian 9. 2. 38 and 9. 3. 24-26).

panied by the whole city together, while each is privately accompanied by his kinsmen.

He calls death "the fated journey" and by "fitting tribute" he means a public funeral procession. Do these periphrases moderately dignify the thought, or do they turn the bare statement into music, as if he poured around it as a harmony the melodious rhythm of the periphrasis? Then Xenophon:

> Hard work you consider to be your guide to a pleasant life. You have stored in your mind the most beautiful of possessions and the most useful in war, for you enjoy praise above all things.

Instead of saying "you are willing to work hard," he says "hard work you consider your guide to a pleasant life" and, by expanding the rest in the same way, he has included a noble idea in his praise. Then there is the inimitable phrase of Herodotus: "The goddess struck those Scythians who robbed her temple with a womanish disease." [1]

29

Yet periphrasis is a hazardous business, more so than other figures; if handled without moderation it at once falls flat, smacks of hollow talk, and becomes heavy. Critics jeer even at Plato (clever as he always is in the use of this figure, he sometimes uses it inappropriately) when he says in the *Laws:* "Neither silver- nor gold-wealth must be allowed to establish itself in our city." [1] If he were forbidding the acquisition of flocks and herds, says the critic, he would obviously have said "sheep-wealth" and "ox-wealth."

This is enough by way of digression about the use of figures as a means to greatness, my dear Terentianus. All these things will make our writing more passionate and exciting; and pas-

---

[1] (28) The three examples of periphrasis are: Plato, *Menexenus* 236d, Xenophon, *Education of Cyrus* 1.5.12, and Herodotus 1.105.4. The "womanish disease" is sexual impotence, the prevalence of which among the Scythians is discussed by Hippocrates, *Airs, Waters, Places,* ch. 22.

[1] (29) Plato, *Laws* 7.801b.

sion is as important in great writing as naturalness [2] is in lighter kinds of writing.

30

Since thought and language usually unfold together, let us now examine some things which remain to be said under the heading of diction. That the choice of words, whether commonplace or grand, wonderfully moves and charms an audience; that it is the chief concern of all speakers and writers; that of itself it endows discourse with grandeur, beauty, mellowness, weight, strength, power, and a certain brightness—qualities also found in the most beautiful statues, providing events, as it were, with a speaking soul—such matters there is no need to discuss with those who know them. Beautiful words are in truth the mind's peculiar light.

To be sure, weighty words are not to be used at all costs, for to clothe petty matters in big and solemn words is like putting a big tragic mask on the face of an infant, except that in poetry . . .

.   .   .   .

31

. . . most satisfying and suggestive, as is the saying of Anacreon: "I care no longer for the Thracian (filly)." [1] This original phrase of Theopompus also deserves praise: "Philip had a talent for stomaching the inevitable"; [2] it is a very significant expression because it fits the facts, though Caecilius, for some reason, condemns it. A vulgarism is sometimes far more expressive than ornamented language; we at once recognize it as drawn from our common experience, and what is

[2] The Greek word is *éthos*. See ch. 9, n. 10.

[1] The fragment is incomplete, the adjective Thracian being feminine and probably contained a pun on filly (*polos*), i.e., filly or girl.

[2] The Greek word for "stomaching the inevitable" is one compound verb—ἀναγκοφαγεῖν.

familiar is more convincing. The expression "to stomach the inevitable" renders the facts very vividly, referring as it does to a man who will, with his own advantage in view, endure what is sordid and ugly with patience and even pleasure. So we find in Herodotus: "Cleomenes in his madness cut his own flesh to bits with his dagger till he mincemeated himself to death." And again: "Pythes fought on in his ships to the moment when he was carved to ribbons." [3] Such expressions verge on vulgarity, but their expressiveness redeems them.

32

As regards the number of metaphors, Caecilius apparently agrees with those who decree that only two, or at most three, should be used in the same passage. Here again we should take Demosthenes as our model. The right time for metaphors is where passion sweeps on like a torrent, carries a large number of them along, and makes them appear necessary. The orator says:

> They are vile flatterers, these men who mutilated each his own land, who toasted away their freedom first to Philip and now to Alexander, who measure happiness by their paunches and their shameless self-indulgence, who have overthrown the liberty and the freedom from despotism which, to the Greeks of earlier days, were the essence and criterion of the good life.[1]

His anger against the traitors eclipses the number of tropes.

Aristotle and Theophrastus say that the boldness of metaphors can be softened by such phrases as "just as if," "such as if," "if one may express it thus," "if one may venture to say so." The apology, they tell us, mitigates the boldness. I accept that but, as I said when dealing with figures, timely and strong passion, as well as genuine greatness, are a special antidote for

[3] The passages from Herodotus are 6. 75. 3 and 7. 181. 1. They are condensed; indeed, Longinus is reminding us of them rather than quoting them, the essential point being one particular phrase in each case.

[1] *On the Crown* 206. The advice attributed to Aristotle in the next paragraph is not found in the Aristotelian corpus.

both the number and the boldness of metaphors. Their swift onrush naturally drives and sweeps everything before them; they make the comparisons appear quite inevitable; and the hearer who shares the inspiration of the speaker is not given time to examine the number of metaphors.

Certainly, nothing is more expressive in the treatment of commonplaces or in descriptions than a succession of metaphors. Xenophon [2] gives us in this way an impressive picture of the anatomy of man's bodily dwelling, and Plato [3] does the same even more divinely. He calls the head the citadel, the neck an isthmus between it and the body. The vertebrae, he says, are fixed under it like pivots; pleasure is a bait of evil for men; the tongue is the assayer of taste; the heart is the knot of the veins and the source of the blood which courses violently round, and it is established in the guardhouse; the passages of the ducts he calls the straits. "As auxiliary support," he says, "for the heart which leaps when anticipating danger or roused to anger (for it is fiery), they implanted the structure of the lungs; it is soft and bloodless, with pores as padding, so that when anger boils up in the heart it should leap against a yielding substance and not be harmed." The seat of passions he called the women's part of the house, and the seat of anger the men's; the spleen is the napkin of the inner parts and, when filled with impurities, it swells and festers. "After this they spread flesh like an awning over it all, making it a protection, like felting, against outside things." The blood he calls the nutriment of the flesh. "And for the sake of nutrition," he says, "they cut channels in the body like watercourses in a garden, so that, as from an incoming river, the body being a porous canal, the streams might flow through the veins." And when the end of death comes, he tells us, the bonds which hold the soul, like a ship's cables, are loosed, and it departs in freedom.

Innumerable expressions of this kind occur in succession. Those we have quoted are enough to show that figurative lan-

[2] *Memorabilia* 1. 4. 5-9.
[3] *Timaeus* 69c ff.

guage has a natural loftiness, that metaphors contribute to great writing, and that they especially delight us in passionate and descriptive passages.

It is obvious even without my mentioning it that the use of tropes, like all beauties of language, always tends to excess. Plato himself is often criticized for this and is said to be driven by a kind of word-frenzy to use immoderate and harsh metaphors and allegorical bombast. For example, he says:

> It is not easy to grasp that a city must be mixed, as the mad seething wine is poured into a mixing bowl and then chastised by another and a sober god. This fine association then produces a good and moderate beverage.[4]

To speak of water as "a sober god" and of mixing as "chastising" is, they say, to speak like a poet who is not sober himself. It is defects such as this which emboldened Caecilius, in his writings on Lysias, to attempt to prove that Lysias is altogether superior to Plato. He is driven to do so by two uncritical passions: he loves Lysias better than he loves himself and he hates Plato even more than he loves Lysias. But he writes in a contentious spirit, and his premises are not as widely accepted as he thought they were. He says the orator is free from blemishes and faultless and prefers him to Plato who has many faults. But this is not the right point of view— far from it.

33

Come, then, let us take one writer who is really free from faults and above criticism. Or should we not discuss this problem in general terms: which is to be preferred in poetry or in prose, great writing with occasional flaws or moderate talent which is entirely sound and faultless? And further, should the prize go to the greater or the more numerous virtues? These questions are very pertinent in a discussion of great writing and they certainly require an answer. I am well aware that supreme genius is certainly not at all free from faults. Precise-

4 *Laws* 6. 772c-d.

ness in every detail incurs the risk of pettiness, whereas with the very great, as with the very rich, something must inevitably be neglected. It is perhaps also inevitable that inferior and average talent remains for the most part safe and faultless because it avoids risk and does not aim at the heights, while great qualities are always precarious because of their very greatness. Nor am I unaware of this further point: that in all human endeavors it is natural for weaknesses to be more easily recognized; the memory of failures remains ineffaceable while successes are easily forgotten.

I have myself drawn attention to not a few faults in Homer and other very great writers. These faults displeased me, yet I did not consider them to be willful mistakes but rather lapses and oversights due to the random carelessness and inattention of genius. In any case, it is my conviction that greater talents, even if not sustained throughout, should get our vote for their nobility of mind if for no other reason. Apollonius is an impeccable poet in the *Argonautica*, and, except for a few externals, Theocritus is equally successful in bucolic poetry, but would you rather be Homer or Apollonius? The *Erigone* of Eratosthenes is a flawless little poem, whereas Archilochus sweeps along with many structural faults but with that outpouring of divine spirit which it is hard to bring under any law. Is Eratosthenes the greater poet? Would you choose to be Bacchylides rather than Pindar in lyric poetry? Or, in tragedy, Ion of Chios rather than Sophocles? The impeccable poets have written with beauty and elegance, but Pindar and Sophocles illumine all things by the flame of their onset, even though that flame is often unaccountably quenched and they sink to a lamentable level. Yet no sane man would count all the plays of Ion to be worth as much as the one play, *Oedipus*.

34

If we judged a writer by the number of good qualities he possesses rather than by their true greatness, Hyperides would be altogether superior to Demosthenes. He has greater variety of tone and more good qualities; like an all-round athlete he is just below the best in each case and the first of the nonspecialists. Besides emulating all the good features of Demosthenes except his word-arrangement, Hyperides also possesses to a high degree the qualities and charm of Lysias. He can speak simply where necessary, not always in a uniform tone like Demosthenes. He has a pleasant and delightful sense of character, with a simple flavor. He has ineffable wit, an urbane sense of ridicule, nobility, a practiced irony, jests neither rude nor vulgar (as was characteristic of the Attic writers of his day) but to the point, adroitness in disparagement, and a stinging, playful, but well-aimed spirit of comedy. All these qualities are enhanced by what we may call an inimitable grace. He has a natural talent for appeals to pity, and for telling a story easily and smoothly to the end, yet he is also very adaptable. His story of Leto is close to poetry, while his funeral oration is as good an example of display oratory as you will find anywhere.

Demosthenes has no sense of character, no easy flow of words; he is not at all smooth, nor good at display. He lacks for the most part all the above-mentioned qualities. Where he forces himself to a jest or a witticism, the audience does not laugh with him so much as at him; when he attempts to attain graceful charm he least achieves it. Had he tried to write the short speech on Phryne or Athenogenes he would have made us favor Hyperides even more. But the fine passages of Hyperides, many as they are, somehow lack greatness; coming "from a sober heart" they fail to move us. No one is awed when reading Hyperides, whereas Demosthenes draws from his noble nature qualities which are completely perfect: the tension of lofty speech, living passion, abundance, alertness of mind, rapidity, and, where needed, an unmatched intensity and power. All these he has drawn to himself like dread gifts from the gods (for they cannot be called human), and by these fine qualities which he does possess he surpasses all men and rises above his deficiencies. He outthunders and outshines the orators of all the ages. His hearers can no more resist the successive outbursts of passion unmoved than gaze with open eyes at a falling thunderbolt.

35

In Plato's case there is, as I said, another difference. He is not deficient in the greatness of his virtues, but rather because they are frequently absent; yet his faults are even more remarkable than the failings of his virtues.[1]

What is it they saw, those godlike writers who in their work aim at what is greatest and overlook precision in every detail? This, among other things: that nature judged man to be no lowly or ignoble creature when she brought us into this life and into the whole universe as into a great celebration, to be spectators of her whole performance and most ambitious actors. She implanted at once into our souls an invincible love for all that is great and more divine than ourselves. That is why the whole universe gives insufficient scope to man's power of contemplation and reflection, but his thoughts often pass beyond the boundaries of the surrounding world. Anyone who looks at life in all its aspects will see how far the remarkable, the great, and the beautiful predominate in all things, and he will soon understand to what end we have been born. That is why, somehow, we are by nature led to marvel, not, indeed, at little streams, clear and useful though they be, but at the Nile, the Danube, or the Rhine, and still more at the Ocean. A little fire which we have lit may keep its flame pure and constant, but it does not awe us more than the fires of heaven, though these may often be obscured; nor do we consider our little fire more worthy of admiration than the craters of Etna whose eruptions throw up

[1] This is the meaning of the MS reading. All translators adopt a very old conjecture which introduces the name of Lysias here and make this passage mean in effect that Lysias is inferior to Plato both in the number of his virtues and in the number of his faults. This is not only pointless, but contradicts the reference to Lysias at the end of ch. 32. It was the fact of *Plato's* faults which led to this whole discussion on the faults of genius. See *AJP* 78 (1957), 371-374.

rocks and mighty boulders or at times pour forth rivers of lava from that single fire within the earth. We might say of all such matters that man can easily understand what is useful or necessary, but he admires what passes his understanding.

36

Therefore, as regards writers of genius whose greatness is ever of use and benefit to us, we should understand at once that, though they are far from being flawless, yet they all reach a more than human level. Other qualities prove writers to be men, greatness raises them close to the nobility of a divine mind. Impeccability escapes all blame, but greatness is the object of our admiration and wonder. What need to add that each of those great writers redeems all his faults by one successful stroke of greatness? If you picked out—and this is the most important point—all the faulty passages in Homer, Demosthenes, Plato, and all the greatest writers, and collected them all together, the result would be small, for the total would not be even a minute fraction of the excellences which these heroes achieve everywhere in their works. That is why the world has, through the ages, granted them the prizes of victory, preserves these prizes to this day, and will continue to do so "while run the flowing waters, and tall trees grow." [1] No madness of envy can challenge that award.

In reply to the writer who denied that the Colossus, with all its faults, is a more powerful work than the Spearman of Polycleitus, one can say, among many other things, that precision is much admired in art but grandeur in the works of nature, and that it is nature which has endowed man with

---

[1] I am a bronzen maiden, on Midas' grave I lie,
    Till stop the flowing waters, and tall trees cease to grow,
    Forever here remaining, on this lamented tomb,
    To those who pass by saying: "Midas is buried here."

The whole epitaph is quoted by Plato in *Phaedrus* 264d as an example of bad art because the lines can be interchanged at will, whereas in a work of art each part should have its proper place and no other, if the whole is to be a true unity.

speech. In statues one seeks for the likeness of a man, but in speech, as I have said, for that which transcends humanity. Nonetheless—and this suggestion takes us back to the beginning of our treatise—since the avoidance of error is mostly due to the successful application of the rules of art while supremacy belongs to genius, it is fitting that art should everywhere give its help to nature. The two together may well produce perfection.

These were the points which needed to be decided in the investigation which we undertook, but everyone may take pleasure in his own views.

37

Akin to metaphors are comparisons and similes; they differ in that . . .

.   .   .   .

38

. . . and this kind: "if you don't wear your brains trampled into your heels." [1] One must know, therefore, how far one can go in each case, for to go too far spoils the hyperbole's effect which, when overstrained, is weakened and may, on occasion, turn into its opposite. Isocrates, for example, is somehow childish in his desire to amplify everything. The theme of his *Panegyric* is that Athens benefited Greece more than Sparta, but he says at once in his introduction:

[1] The phrase occurs at the end of Demosthenes' speech *On Halonnesus* (45) where he tells his fellow citizens that they should liquidate any Athenians who are friendly to Philip "if you carry your brains in your head and not trampled into your heels" (the quotation, as so often, is condensed). Because of the lacuna it is not quite clear whether Longinus disapproves of the expression but it would seem so, and indeed the whole speech was thought to be spurious even in antiquity partly because of this phrase, which certainly insults the audience in a more violent and less successful way than is customary in Demosthenes.

The power of words is such that it can make great things small and endow small things with greatness; it can present old events in a new way, or describe in a timeworn manner things that have recently happened.[2]

One might well ask him: "Do you then, Isocrates, intend to alter the parts played by the Spartans and the Athenians?" For his eulogy of the power of words makes the introduction almost a warning to his readers that he himself is not to be trusted. What we said earlier about figures is also true here: the best hyperboles are sometimes those which are not noticed to be hyperboles at all. This happens when, under the stress of strong emotion, they help to express a certain grandeur in the situation, as Thucydides does in the case of those killed in Sicily:

> The Syracusans came down and began to massacre them in the river. The water was immediately soiled, but they drank it nonetheless, bloodied and muddy, and many of them still fought to get at it.[3]

That blood and mud were drunk and fought for is made credible by the extreme emotional tension of the moment. Herodotus does much the same thing in his description of the battle of Thermopylae:

> They defended themselves with their daggers, if they still had them, with their hands, with their teeth, as they were buried under Persian missiles.[4]

Here you may well ask what kind of defense one can make with one's teeth against fully armed men, and what is this burying with missiles? But it carries conviction because the circumstances are not described to justify the hyberbole, rather the hyperbole arises reasonably from the circumstances. As I

[2] We should note that Longinus uses the term hyperbole in a rather wide sense, for certainly this passage from Isocrates (*Panegyric* 8) is hardly a hyperbole in the usual sense but at most an exaggeration. Here again, however, the lacuna makes things uncertain.

[3] Thucydides 7. 84. 5.

[4] Herodotus 7. 225. 3. This is true hyperbole, but the passage from Thucydides seems hardly an exaggeration.

never cease repeating, actions and passions which bring one close to distraction compensate for and justify every boldness of expression. So, too, comic hyperboles, though they overstep the limit of credibility, are convincing because of the laughter they arouse, as in: "His field was shorter than a Spartan's letter"; for laughter, too, is a passion which has its roots in pleasure. Hyperbole may exaggerate the small as well as the large, for exaggeration may be in either direction, and ridicule is an amplification of the paltry side of things.

39

The fifth of those elements which we mentioned at the beginning as contributing to greatness still remains to be considered, my friend—namely, the arrangement of words. I have adequately presented my conclusions on this subject in two published works. This much, however, I should add here—namely, that a sense of melody is not only inborn in man as a means of persuasion and delight, but it is also a marvelous instrument when allied to a free flow of passion.

Does not the music of the flute stir the emotions of an audience, take them out of themselves, fill them with Corybantic frenzy,[1] and by its rhythmic beat compel him who hears it to step to its rhythm and identify himself with its tune, even if he be quite unmusical? Yes, in truth it does, and the notes of the lyre, though they express no meaning, often cast a marvelous spell, as you know, by variations of sound, by their rapid succession, and by the mingling of their concords. Yet these are but images and bastard imitations of persuasion and not, as I said, among the nobler pursuits which specifically belong to our human nature. Shall we then not believe that the arrangement of words—that music of rational speech which is in man inborn, which appeals not to the ear only but to the mind itself—as it evokes a variety of words, thoughts, events, and beautiful melodies, all of them born with us and

---

[1] The Corybantes were the eunuch priests of Cybele, the Asiatic Earth-Mother, whose rites were notorious for their wild, ecstatic nature.

bred into us, instills the speaker's feelings, by the blended variety of its sounds, into the hearts of those near him so that they share his passions? It charms us by the architecture of its phrases as it builds the music of great passages which casts a spell upon us and at the same time ever disposes us to dignity, honor, greatness, and all the qualities it holds within itself.

Perhaps it is foolish even to question matters so generally accepted, for experience is sufficient proof. Great and wonderful is the thought which Demosthenes expressed when speaking of his proposal: "This decree caused the danger which then threatened our city to pass away like a cloud," [2] and the word-music is no less remarkable than the thought. The whole sentence has a generally dactylic effect, that noblest and greatest rhythm which is the basis of the heroic hexameter. Transpose any word and you will realize how word-music chimes in unison with greatness. Say, for example: "This decree has caused the danger, which like a cloud threatened our city, to pass away." Or if you cut off one single syllable and, for example, use ὡς for ὥσπερ (– for – –) in the last phrase, the difference is even greater. The original expression ὥσπερ νέφος (– – ∪ ∪) starts with a long rhythm of two long syllables, equivalent in time to four shorts. Delete one syllable and the excision at once mutilates the greatness of the sentence. Then again, if you lengthen the phrase by one syllable and say ὥσπερεὶ νέφος (– ∪ – ∪ ∪), the meaning is the same but it strikes the ear quite differently: the abrupt greatness of the sentence is lost and the pace is slackened by the longer rhythm at the end.

40

Among the factors which give most dignity to discourse is structure, which corresponds to the arrangement of the limbs of the body. One limb by itself, cut off from the others, is of no value, but all of them together complete and perfect the composition of the whole. So it is with great expressions: scattered here and there, apart from each other, they lose

2 *On the Crown* 188.

their own value and undo the greatness of the whole, but when they form a whole in close association, joined together by the bonds of melodious word-arrangement, then in the rounded structure of the whole they find their voice. A great work is like a feast to the courses of which many people contribute.[1]

We have had sufficient proof that a good many writers of prose and poetry who have no natural genius—often, indeed, no great inborn talent—use commonplace, popular words, and, as a rule, no unusual language; yet by the mere arrangement and harmonizing of these words they endow their work with dignity, distinction, and the appearance of not being ordinary. After the murder of his children, Heracles says:

I have my load of ills, none can be added.[2]

The idea is thoroughly commonplace, but the line becomes great because the word-arrangement suits the image. If you arrange the words differently, you will see at once that Euripides is a poet in the arrangement of his words rather than in the quality of his mind. He says of Dirce dragged away by the bull:

And if he chanced
To twist or turn, he dragged along as one
The oak, the rock, the woman, intertwined.

Here the idea is grand, too, but it is made more forceful by the arrangement of the words which move slowly and are not, one might say, carried along on rollers; the collocation of sounds makes pauses inevitable between them. These support the long syllables with an effect of stable, wide-stepping grandeur.

---

[1] The Greek word *periodos* is not used in the technical sense of "period" by Longinus, whereas, in conjunction with the word *eranos*—a feast to which each contributes—the meaning of courses going around is quite natural. The usual translation "in the periods" makes very poor sense, for what Longinus says here has nothing to do with periodic structure, which he never mentions. See *AJP* 78 (1957), 368-370.

[2] Euripides, *Heracles* 1245. The following quotation is from a lost play of the same author.

41

There is nothing so detrimental to great passages as for the prose to have a broken, hurried rhythm. Meters of this kind are the pyrrhic ($\cup\cup$), the trochee ($-\cup$), and the double trochee ($-\cup-\cup$), for in the end they turn into dance rhythms. Overrhythmical passages at once seem precious, petty, passionless, and shallow because of their monotonous patterns. And the worst feature of all is that, like chansonnettes, they draw the reader's attention away from what is being said and divert it to the rhythm itself. In this way exaggerated rhythms do not communicate to the hearer the emotion appropriate to the subject but that which is evoked by the rhythm. The audience, foreseeing the rhythmical clause that is to come, beats time for the speaker and, as in a choral dance, calls out the metrical ending before he reaches it. Equally devoid of dignity are excessively compact phrases cut up into little short-syllabled clauses which are then, as it were, clamped together by strong bolts over the fissures and harshnesses between.

42

Another factor which diminishes greatness is excessively concise language, for grandeur is maimed when forced into too small a mold. I do not mean unnecessary compactness but a continuous succession of small bits of sentences. Such shortened clauses break the sequence of thought, whereas brevity goes straight to the point. On the other hand, prolixity, length which the occasion does not require, is clearly deadening.

43

The use of trivial words is very apt to disfigure great passages. Herodotus' description of a storm, for example, is marvelously conceived, but it contains some expressions which are quite unworthy of the subject matter. For instance "the sea was sizzling": the word "sizzling" strips the phrase of greatness because of its ugly sound. "The wind," he says, "was worn out" and "a disagreeable end" awaited those clinging to the wreckage. "To be worn out" is a colloquialism without dignity and "disagreeable" does not belong to such an experience.[1]

Similarly Theopompus, after magnificently describing the descent of the Persian into Egypt, spoils the whole thing by a few petty words:

> What city, what tribe from all Asia was not represented before the king? What, of all the beautiful works of nature or precious perfections of art, was not brought as a present to him? Were there not many expensive coverlets and cloaks, some purple, some embroidered, some white; many pavilions of gold furnished with all that was useful, many robes and costly couches? Further, plate of silver and wrought gold, goblets and mixing bowls studded with precious stones or finely and luxuriously engraved. All this you might have seen, and, besides, untold myriads of weapons from Greece and Barbary, countless beasts of burden and victims fatted for the kill; many bushels of condiments, many bags, sacks, and sheets of papyrus and all manner of useful things; so many pieces of salted meat from all kinds of sacrificial animals in such great heaps that those who approached from a distance thought they were faced by a succession of mounds and hills.

He deserts the greater for the more humble, whereas amplification should proceed the other way round. Into his wonderful account of the whole he injects bags and condiments and sacks, thus awakening a picture of a kitchen. Just as if, in real life, between all those grand ornaments of gold, stone-inlaid bowls, silver plate, solid gold pavilions and goblets, one were to introduce, right in the middle of them, bags and sacks, the result would be uncouth to the eye; so also words like these, introduced at the wrong time, are a disfigurement and a blot upon the style.

He could have given a general description as he tells of the mounds piled up, and thus have spoken, in the rest of the

[1] The expressions criticized are found in Herodotus 7. 188. 2 and 191. 2; 8. 13.

display, of chariots and camels and the mass of beasts of burden bringing everything that can contribute to the luxurious enjoyments of the table; or he could have mentioned heaps of every kind of plant, and especially those which excel for cookery and enjoyment; or, if he wanted to make the list complete, all the refinements of butlers and cooks. In great passages one must not drop to the sordid and the outrageous unless under strong compulsion, but the words should be worthy of the subject and imitate nature when she fashioned man. She did not put our unmentionable parts or the drainage system of the whole body on our faces, but she hid them as best she could. As Xenophon said, she placed these channels away as far as possible, thus in no way marring the beauty of the whole creature.[2] There is no need to enumerate every species of triviality. As we have now pointed out the qualities which make writing noble and great, so, obviously, it will be the opposite qualities which, for the most part, make it low and unseemly.

44

There is one further matter, and, since you, my dear Terentianus, are an eager student of literature, I shall not hesitate to add to our study a clarification of the question which one of the philosophers was very recently investigating: "I wonder," he said, "as assuredly many people do, why it is that, while there is today no dearth of men who are persuasive, interested in public affairs, shrewd, skillful, and certainly delightful speakers, our age so very rarely produces men of outstanding genius. A world-wide sterility of utterance has come upon our life. Must we indeed accept," he continued, "the well-worn cliché that democracy is a good foster mother of greatness, that great speakers flourished when she flourished and died with her? Freedom, they say, is able to nurture the thoughts of great minds and to give them hope; with it comes eagerness to compete and ambition to grasp the highest rewards. Because of the prizes available in free cities, the nat-

[2] *Memorabilia* 1. 4. 5-9.

ural talents of speakers are trained, sharpened, polished as it were by practice, and they shine forth in the free handling of affairs. In our own day," he said, "we learn righteous slavery as children, we are all but swaddled in its customs and practices while our minds are still tender; we have never tasted of the most beautiful and most creative spring of language. By this I mean freedom," he said, "and so we turn out to have no genius except for flattery." He went on to say that a slave can have many other qualities, but he can never be an orator. His lack of freedom to speak wells up in him and stands guard like a watchman made fearful by habitual thrashings. As Homer said: "The day of slavery makes one but half a man." [1] "Indeed," he said, "as in the case of the dwarfs whom we call Pygmies, not only do the cages in which they are kept stunt their growth, but their bonds, if I am rightly informed, actually make their bodies shrink, so slavery of every kind, even the best, could be shown to be the cage and common prisonhouse of the soul."

To this I replied: "It is easy, my good sir, and very human, always to blame the circumstances of the times; but consider: perhaps it is not the peace of the world which destroys great talents, but much more so this endless war which occupies our passions and, beyond that, the desires which surely rule our present world like an army of occupation and drive absolutely everything before them.

"We are the slaves of money, which is an insatiable disease in us all, and also the slaves of pleasure; these two violate our lives and our persons. The love of gold is a disease which shrinks a man, and the love of pleasure is ignoble. And, as I think on it, I cannot see how we can honor wealth without limit or, and this is nearer the truth, make it our god, without admitting into our souls those kindred evils that inevitably follow it. Wealth unmeasured and unchecked is closely accompanied step by step by extravagance; once wealth has opened the gates of the city or the home, extravagance steps in and they settle down together. In time, as the wise tell us, they build their nest in our lives and swiftly turn to breeding

1 *Odyssey* 17.322.

their young; they give birth to selfishness and to vanity and to luxuriousness, no bastard children these but their true offspring. If then one leaves these children of riches to grow to maturity, they quickly breed ruthless tyrants in our souls: violence, lawlessness, and shamelessness. This happens inevitably; then men no longer look upward nor care for later fame. Little by little the corruption of life's circle is completed; great qualities of soul wither, waste away, and are no longer esteemed; and men come to admire what is mortal within them, for they have neglected the growth of the immortal.

"When once a man has been bribed to give judgment, he can never again be a free and healthy judge of the right and the beautiful, for he who has been bribed inevitably conceives his own interest to be both beautiful and right. When bribes direct the whole life of each of us throughout, when we chase after the deaths of others and ambush legacies, we find monetary gain everywhere and this we buy, each at the cost of his own soul. Then we are slaves. Can we believe that in this pestilence and corruption of life there is left any free, unbribed judge of greatness and of the things that will reach ages to come, and that he will not be outvoted by the corrupt practices of selfishness? Perhaps it is better for men such as we are to be ruled than to be free. For surely if our selfish desires were altogether freed from prison, as it were, and let loose upon our neighbors, they would scorch the earth with their evils.

"In a word," I said, "the worst bane of all those born now is the indifference in which, with rare exceptions, all of us live, never laboring or undertaking anything for its own sake, but only for praise or pleasure, never for any benefit worthy of honor or emulation." " 'T were best to let this in confusion be," [2] and to proceed to our next topic. This was emotions or passions, which we earlier promised to treat as the main topic of a separate work. They have a place in the rest of our discussions and certainly in great writing . . . .

2 From Euripides, *Electra* 379.

BIOGRAPHICAL INDEX

ACHILLES, Greek hero of the *Iliad*. Insulted by Agamemnon, he refuses to fight until aroused by the death of his friend Patroclus. He then savagely kills the Trojan champion, Hector.

AESCHINES (*c.* 390-325 B.C.), Athenian orator who favored Philip of Macedon. He was the chief opponent of Demosthenes.

AESCHYLUS (525-456 B.C.), the eldest of the three great Athenian writers of tragedies. His tragedies raise deep religious and human problems. The tempo and language of his plays were already archaic in the late fifth century B.C.

AGAMEMNON, commander in chief of Greek forces before Troy in the *Iliad*.

AGATHOCLES (361-289 B.C.), ruler of Syracuse, engaged in prolonged wars against Carthage.

AJAX, Greek hero in the *Iliad*. Sophocles in the *Ajax* dramatized the later legend of his madness and suicide after the arms of the dead Achilles were awarded to Odysseus.

ALCAEUS (b. *c.* 620 B.C.), a contemporary of Sappho in Lesbos and a writer of passionate personal lyrics.

ALEXANDER THE GREAT (356-323 B.C.), son of Philip of Macedon, conquered all of Asia as far as the Indus and greatly helped to spread Greek culture to the East.

ALOADAE, in legend Otus and Ephialtes, giant sons of Aloeus. They attacked the gods on Olympus by piling mountain on mountain. They were destroyed by Zeus.

AMMONIUS (2nd c. B.C.), pupil of Aristarchus and literary scholar of distinction who wrote on Plato's debt to Homer.

AMMONIUS SACCAS (3rd c. A.D.), a teacher of mystic philosophy at Alexandria. Plotinus and Longinus were his students.

AMPHICRATES, a little-known Athenian rhetorician of the late second or early first century B.C.

ANACREON of Teos (b. *c.* 570 B.C.), famous lyric poet, writer of hymns, love songs, and convivial poetry.

APOLLONIUS of Rhodes (b. *c.* 295 B.C.), author of the *Argonautica*, a still extant epic in four books on the quest of the Golden Fleece.

APSINES of Gadara (*c.* A.D. 190-250), teacher of rhetoric at Athens.

ARATUS (*c.* 315-240 B.C.), Greek poet. His best-known work is an astronomical poem in hexameters, the *Phainomena*, which is extant.

ARCHILOCHUS of Paros (late 8th c. B.C.?), one of the early Greek lyric poets, also renowned for his lampoons in iambic meter.

ARES, the god of battle, always rather an "outsider" on Olympus.

ARISTARCHUS of Samothrace (c. 217-145 B.C.), head of the museum library in Alexandria, literary scholar, editor, and commentator, often called "the founder of scientific scholarship."

ARISTEAS of Proconnesus, of uncertain date, reputed author of an epic on the legendary Arimaspeans.

ARISTOTLE (384-322 B.C.), Greek philosopher, pupil of Plato. His extant works (many are lost) cover most aspects of philosophy. His *Poetics* had tremendous influence over the critical theories of the Renaissance (it was lost in antiquity), while his *Rhetoric* contains most of the basic principles of ancient literary criticism.

ARRIAN (2nd c. A.D.), Roman officer of Greek origin. He wrote the *Enchiridion* and *Discourses* of the Stoic philosopher Epictetus and histories of Eastern countries, including the *Anabasis* on the conquests of Alexander the Great.

ATHENA, patron goddess of Athens, daughter of Zeus. In the epics she favored the Greeks before Troy and Odysseus throughout his adventures.

ATHENOGENES, an Egyptian resident in Athens of whom noth-ing is known except what can be gathered from Hyperides' fragmentary speech against him.

BACCHYLIDES of Ceos (5th c. B.C.), was a famous Greek lyric poet of whose work considerable fragments remain.

CADMUS, legendary founder of Thebes.

CAECILIUS of Calacte, rhetorician teaching in Rome in the late first century B.C., only fragments of whose critical works on Greek orators remain. His treatise on *Hypsos* evoked Longinus' *On the Sublime*.

CALLISTHENES (4th c. B.C.), Greek historian, nephew of Aristotle. He accompanied Alexander the Great to the East, but was executed for conspiring against him.

CASSANDRA, daughter of Priam, king of Troy. She was endowed by Apollo with the gift of prophecy but, because she resisted him, her prophecies were never to be believed.

CEYX, in legend king of Trachis and friend of Heracles.

CICERO, MARCUS TULLIUS (106-43 B.C.), Roman statesman, philosopher, and orator, the apostle of Roman humanism. His philosophical works popularized Greek philosophy in Latin and had tremendous influence on Western thought. His works on rhetoric embody his ideal of culture and education and preserved much of Greek theory.

CIRCE, daughter of the Sun who turned Odysseus' companions

into swine. Odysseus escaped with the help of Hermes (*Odyssey* 10).

CLEITARCHUS (3rd c. B.C.), Alexandrian historian who wrote on Alexander the Great.

CLEOMENES I, king of Sparta *c.* 519-487 B.C. He died in a fit of madness.

COLOSSUS may refer to any statue of more than life size. The reference (ch. 36) is perhaps to the famous bronze Colossus of Rhodes.

CYCLOPS, the man-eating, one-eyed giant blinded by Odysseus in the ninth book of the *Odyssey*.

CYRUS II, younger son of Darius, king of Persia, revolted against his brother Artaxerxes II in 401 B.C. and was defeated and killed at Cunaxa. He was much admired by Xenophon.

DARIUS I, king of Persia 521-486 B.C. at the time of the Ionian revolt and of the first Greco-Persian war. He was the great organizer of the Persian empire.

DEMETRIUS of Phalerum (b. *c.* 350 B.C.), an Athenian pupil of Theophrastus who ruled Athens for the Macedonian king Cassander 317-307 B.C. and later lived in Alexandria. He was formerly considered the author of an extant treatise *On Style*, now thought to be of uncertain date and authorship.

DEMOSTHENES (384-322 B.C.), the greatest of Greek orators and the passionate defender of Athens against Philip of Macedon. Many of his political and judicial speeches are extant.

DIOMEDE, in the *Iliad* leader of the Argive contingent and second among the Greeks only to Achilles.

DION (*c.* 408-354 B.C.), friend of Plato who sought the philosopher's help to convert Dionysius II of Syracuse to philosophy. He finally ousted the "tyrant" and ruled Syracuse for a time.

DIONYSIUS II (4th c. B.C.) succeeded his father as ruler of Syracuse in 367 B.C. Plato tried vainly to make a philosopher-king of him.

DIONYSIUS of Halicarnassus (1st c. B.C.), Greek rhetorician and historian, lived in Rome 30-8 B.C. Many of his critical works are extant, the most original and important being his *On Composition* (i.e., word-arrangement). He is the author also of a history of early Rome, *Roman Antiquities,* of which half is extant.

DIONYSIUS of Phocaea, leader of the contingent from that city at the battle of Lade in 494 B.C., when the Asiatic Greeks were defeated by the Persians.

DIONYSUS, son of Zeus and Semele, god of wine and ecstasy and patron of the drama. Dramatic performances were held at festivals in his honor.

DIRCE was, in legend, tied to the horns of a wild bull by Amphion and Zethus, sons of

Zeus, as punishment for her cruelty to their mother Antiope.

ENYO, spirit and goddess of war.

ERATOSTHENES (*c.* 275-194 B.C.), Greek scholar, was more famous as a geographer, scholar, and polymath than as a poet. His works are lost.

EUNAPIUS (A.D. 346-414), a Lydian Greek, historian and author of the extant *Lives of the Philosophers and Sophists.*

EUPOLIS (fl. 430-410 B.C.), Athenian writer of comedies, contemporary of Aristophanes.

EURIPIDES (*c.* 485-406 B.C.), the third of the three great tragedians. Often called the philosopher of the stage. His eighteen extant plays reflect the thought and questionings of his day.

EURYLOCHUS, companion of Odysseus in the *Odyssey.*

FURIES or ERINYES, also called by the propitiating name of Eumenides (the kindly ones), were primeval spirits avenging murder, especially of kindred.

GORGIAS of Leontini (5th c. B.C.), famous Sophist and teacher of rhetoric who visited Athens in 427 B.C. and introduced the Athenians to Sicilian rhetorical devices. His influence on Greek prose style was great, though he was ridiculed for his excesses by Aristotle and later critics.

HADES, god of the underworld and brother of Zeus.

HECATAEUS of Miletus (fl. 500 B.C.), historian and geographer.

Only fragments of his works remain.

HECTOR, in the *Iliad* a son of Priam and leader of the Trojans who was slain by Achilles.

HEGESIAS of Magnesia (fl. *c.* 250 B.C.), Greek rhetorician, is regarded by critics as the foremost practitioner of the "Asiatic," i.e., florid and excessively rhythmical, style which was developed in his day.

HELIOS, mythical god of the Sun, represented as a charioteer.

HERACLES, legendary hero, son of Zeus and the mortal Alcmene. In the performance of his twelve labors, he became the symbol of laboring humanity.

HERACLIDAE, the sons (and later descendants) of Heracles.

HERACLIDES (4th c. B.C.) helped Dion against Dionysius II of Syracuse. Later he opposed Dion and was murdered.

HERMES, messenger of the gods, himself the god of trickery. He is also connected with fertility.

HERMOCRATES (5th c. B.C.), Syracusan general who helped to defeat the Athenian expedition against Syracuse in 415 B.C.

HERMOGENES of Tarsus (b. *c.* A.D. 150) wrote Greek technical treatises on rhetoric which were commented on throughout later antiquity and are still extant.

HERODOTUS (5th c. B.C.), the first great Greek historian, author of a *History* in nine books of the Greek struggle against Persia.

HESIOD, Greek poet of unknown date, but later than Homer. He wrote hexameter didactic poetry: *Works and Days*, a farmer's calendar interspersed with moral advice, and the *Theogony*, birth and function of all the gods. A short epic on *The Shield of Achilles* was also attributed to him.

HIPPOCRATES (5th c. B.C.), the father of Greek medicine. Many medical writings attributed to him are extant.

HOMER, author of the two great epics of Greece, the *Iliad* and the *Odyssey*. We know nothing of Homer, or whether there was one Homer who united all the epic lays into the two great poems. His date is variously thought to be 800 B.C. or within a century either way. But he was *the* poet for two thousand years to all Greek writers, and his stories (in translation) are still best-sellers today.

HORACE (QUINTUS HORATIUS FLACCUS, 65-8 B.C.), Roman poet, writer of the famous odes. He also wrote iambic epodes and hexameter satires and letters. One of these is his *Art of Poetry*.

HYPERIDES (389-332 B.C.), Attic orator, contemporary of Demosthenes, whom he generally supported.

IOCASTA, in Theban legend mother and wife of Oedipus.

ION of Chios (b. *c.* 490 B.C.) wrote tragedies in Athens, as well as other kinds of poetry. Nothing of his work remains.

ISOCRATES (436-338 B.C.) taught rhetoric in Athens for over fifty years, the most influential teacher of his day. To him education meant the capacity to speak well on great subjects. He was a most careful stylist, especially notorious for avoidance of hiatus. Because he could not speak in public, his "speeches" are really pamphlets; many of them are extant.

LETO, goddess mother of Apollo and Artemis by Zeus.

LYCURGUS, mythological king of the Edoni who opposed the religion of Dionysus.

LYSIAS (*c.* 459-*c.* 380 B.C.), an Athenian orator famous for the natural simplicity of his style. He became the model of those who wished to return to Attic simplicity in Roman times.

MATRIS (late 3rd c. B.C.?), Theban orator, an exponent of the florid, "Asiatic" style.

MEGILLUS, one of the speakers in Plato's *Laws*, a Spartan. The others are Cleinias, a Cretan, and an unnamed Athenian (Plato himself).

ODYSSEUS, a Greek hero in the *Iliad*. The *Odyssey* is the story of his adventures on his return from Troy to his home in Ithaca. Always the type of clever, resourceful man, he was harshly dealt with by the tragedians and later legend.

OEDIPUS, in legend the son of Laius, king of Thebes. In fulfillment of a prophecy, he unknowingly killed his father and married the widowed queen Iocasta, his mother.

ORESTES, in legend the son of Agamemnon and Clytemnestra. Orestes was a child when Clytemnestra killed Agamemnon on his return from Troy. He later killed his mother to avenge his father, and was maddened by the Furies.

PARMENIO (c. 400-330 B.C.), general under Philip of Macedon and his son, Alexander the Great.

PATROCLUS, Greek hero and friend of Achilles in the *Iliad*.

PELOPS, in legend the son of Tantalus and grandfather of Agamemnon.

PENELOPE, wife of Odysseus in the *Odyssey*. She is courted by many suitors whom she puts off.

PETRONIUS (1st c. A.D.), at one time favorite of Nero. He wrote the *Satiricon*, a satirical picaresque novel only very partially extant.

PHAETHON, the son of Helios, the Sun. He tried to drive his father's chariot and was killed by Zeus.

PHILIP II (382-336 B.C.), king of Macedon from 359. He gradually brought the Greek cities under his control and made possible the conquests of his son Alexander the Great.

PHRYNE (4th c. B.C.), Athenian courtesan defended by Hyperides when charged with impiety.

PHRYNICHUS (5th c. B.C.), Athenian writer of tragedies. He produced a play on the capture of Miletus in 494 B.C. by the Persians and was fined.

PINDAR (518-438 B.C.), Boeotian lyric poet. Many of his odes celebrating victories in athletic contests are extant. He is recognized as one of the great poets of Greece.

PLATO (429-347 B.C.), disciple of Socrates and teacher of Aristotle, founder of the Academy which survived till all pagan schools were closed in A.D. 529. He was not only a great philosopher but a very great literary artist. His dialogues show an infinite variety of style not always appreciated by ancient critics. His own criticisms of poetry and rhetoric are found in the *Republic*, the *Phaedrus*, and the second book of the *Laws*.

PLOTINUS (A.D. 205-269), Roman philosopher, originator of Neo-Platonism, a kind of mystical Platonism. He was the author of the *Enneads*, edited by Porphyry and extant.

PLUTARCH (c. A.D. 46-127) of Chaeronea, philosophizing scholar and moralist. He wrote many essays on moral and literary subjects and the famous *Lives* of the great men of Greece and Rome.

POLYCLEITUS (fl. 450-405 B.C.), a famous Greek sculptor, native of Argos.

PORPHYRY (A.D. 232-c. 305), disciple of Plotinus, editor of his *Enneads*. A Neo-Platonist, he was a voluminous writer on philosophy and religion and an opponent of Christianity.

POSEIDON, god of the sea, brother of Zeus. His hostility followed Odysseus throughout his wanderings.

PYTHES, a man from Aegina who displayed great heroism when his ship was surprised by the Persians (480 B.C.). He was captured alive and later freed by the Greeks. (Herod. 7. 181 and 8. 182.)

QUINTILIAN (MARCUS FABIUS QUINTILIANUS, c. A.D. 35-100), Spanish-born Roman teacher of rhetoric and author of *Institutio oratoria* (i.e., the education of the orator), a definitive work in twelve books on Greco-Roman education and rhetorico-literary theories.

SAPPHO (b. c. 612 B.C.) of Lesbos, the most famous love-poetess of antiquity.

SARPEDON, in the *Iliad* leader of the Lycians in the defense of Troy. He is killed by Patroclus.

SENECA (c. 55 B.C.–c. A.D. 40), the father of the better-known philosopher, tragedian, and minister of Nero. He wrote for his sons a collection of reminiscences of the rhetorical schools, *Controversiae et Suasoriae*.

SIMONIDES (c. 556-468 B.C.), a famous lyric poet.

SOCRATES (469-399 B.C.), Athenian philosopher, the true originator of ethical philosophy. He wrote nothing but spent his life exhorting the Athenians to live the good life. He emphasized the Delphic advice, "Know thyself," and believed that virtue was knowledge and vice was ignorance. Brought to trial for atheism and "corrupting the young," he was put to death. Socrates' influence was immense and Plato was his greatest follower.

SOPHOCLES (c. 496-406 B.C.), perhaps the greatest poet of the three great tragedians of Athens. Seven of his plays remain.

STESICHORUS (c. 630-555 B.C.) of Himera in Sicily, a famous writer of lyric poetry with a strong narrative element.

TACITUS (c. A.D. 55-120), Roman historian of the early Empire in his *Annals, Histories,* and *Agricola.* He is also the author of a *Dialogue on Orators.*

THEOCRITUS of Syracuse (c. 310-250 B.C.), writer of pastoral idyls, a number of which are extant.

THEODORUS of Gadara (fl. 33 B.C.), head of a rhetorical school in opposition to Apollodorus of Pergamum. Theodorus seems to have been less rigid in the application of rhetorical rules.

THEOPHRASTUS (c. 372-288 B.C.), Greek philosopher, successor of Aristotle as head of the

Lyceum. His works on criticism and rhetoric are lost.

THEOPOMPUS of Chios (b. *c.* 378 B.C.), pupil of Isocrates, wrote many works on Greek history. Only fragments remain.

THUCYDIDES (*c.* 460-400 B.C.), author of the famous history of the Peloponnesian War between Athens and Sparta (431-404 B.C.) and considered the originator of scientific history.

TIMAEUS of Taurumenium (*c.* 356-260 B.C.), studied rhetoric in Athens and wrote a history of Sicily in thirty-eight books.

XENOPHON (*c.* 430-*c.* 354 B.C.), friend of Socrates, soldier, country gentleman, and author of historical, Socratic, and moral works.

XERXES I, king of Persia 485-465 B.C. at the time of the second Persian War. He threw a bridge over the Hellespont and dug a canal through the Athos peninsula to get his army to Greece.

ZEUS, the most powerful of the gods, brother of Hera, Hades, and Poseidon, father of the other gods.

ZOÏLUS (4th c. B.C.), a Cynic philosopher who bitterly attacked Homer. His criticisms, which seem to us negative and petty, earned him the nickname of Homeromastix, "the scourge of Homer."